GET OUT

OF THAT

PIT

GET OUT OF THAT PIT

Straight Talk
about God's
Deliverance

FROM A FORMER PIT-DWELLER

BETH MOORE

THOMAS NELSON
Since 1798

NASHVILLE   DALLAS   MEXICO CITY   RIO DE JANEIRO   BEIJING

Published in Nashville, Tennessee, by Thomas Nelson. Thomas Nelson is a registered trademark of Thomas Nelson, Inc.

Published in association with Yates & Yates, LLP, www.yates2.com.

Thomas Nelson, Inc. titles may be purchased in bulk for educational, business, fund-raising, or sales promotional use. For information, please e-mail SpecialMarkets@ThomasNelson.com.

Unless otherwise indicated, Scripture quotations are taken from The Holy Bible, New International Version®. ©1973, 1978, 1984, by International Bible Society. Used by permission of Zondervan. All rights reserved.

Other scripture quotations are taken from: The Amplified Bible (AMP). © 1954, 1958, 1962, 1964, 1965, 1987 by The Lockman Foundation. Used by permission. All rights reserved. The American Standard Version (ASV). Public domain. The Holy Bible, English Standard Version (ESV). © 2001 by Crossway Bibles, a division of Good News Publishers. Used by permission. All rights reserved. The Holman Christian Standard Bible® (HCSB). © 1999, 2000, 2002, 2003 by Holman Bible Publishers. Used by permission. The King James Version (KJV). Public domain. The New American Standard Bible® (NASB®). © 1960, 1962, 1963, 1968, 1971, 1972, 1973, 1975, 1977, 1995 by The Lockman Foundation. Used by permission. The New King James Version® (NKJV®). © 1982 by Thomas Nelson, Inc. Used by permission. All rights reserved.

ISBN 978-0-7852-8973-9 (trade paper)

Library of Congress Cataloging-in-Publication Data
Moore, Beth, 1957–
    Get out of that pit / Beth Moore.
        p. cm.
    Summary:"Helpful lessons for those who feel like they live in a state of confusion"—Provided by publisher.
    Includes bibliographical references.
    ISBN 978-1-59145-552-3 (hardcover)
    1. Christian life. I. Title.
BV4501.3.M6542 2007
248.8'6—dc22

                                    2006033446

Printed in the United States of America
10 11 12 RRD 11 10 9 8

To the Tates and the Weirs,
For resisting a handful of overwhelming temptations to the pit and
trusting the unseen hand of God instead.
Thank you for making me feel like part of your family and
inviting me into countless tender moments.
I am the better for knowing all of you.

And especially to my beloved Kendall,
Who refuses to waste a moment of life—no matter how hard—in a pit.
You, Darling One, are my hero. Miss Beth loves you so much.

Contents

Acknowledgments

I have never recovered from the grace God has had on my messed up life. I have had a life long struggle with seeing value in myself but I can see tremendous value in those He's brought along to partner with me in ministry. One way God has dealt with that handicapped part of me is to show me the excellence and holy passion of those who have been willing to work with me. In that strange round about way, God has shown me that, if people like them are willing to pour their time and energy into that project or ministry, God must be up to something worth something.

The list of hands to this plough is long. It also turned out to be an emotionally expensive project as most of the primary investors in all the areas necessary to editing and publishing were allowed by God to experience the message through an uncanny invitation to a pit of their own. We were able to resist because God faithfully equipped us and, in the process, we became more and more passionate about this message. Life is one invitation to the pit after another. That's all there is to it. That's why I thank you so much, Rob Birkhead, Betty Wood-mancy, Barb James, Kris Bearss, Jennifer Day, Amy Williams, and Scott Harris for making sure this message gets into the hands of the people, and Laura Kendall for writing the discovery guide questions that will help people get involved.

Jeana Ledbetter, my beloved friend, you took the hardest hit of all as these concepts were tested on us and you resisted best of all. No one worked harder on this project. You are an excellent woman and Christ is surely so taken with you. We are bonded for life.

Sealy Yates, you are my good buddy. Trustworthy indeed. I'm crazy about you. Your emails always turn into daily devotionals for me.

Joey Paul and Byron Williamson, you stole my heart when you threw every effort and took every risk a missionary book like *Voices of the Faithful* poses. You are my dear brothers in Christ. As Sealy and Jeana can well attest, I never had any intention of publishing this book with anyone else. This is a Beth, Joey, Byron book.

Tom Williams and Leslie Peterson, thank you for your excellent editorial work. It's a much better book because of you. And thank you for not taking a chainsaw to my annoying conversational style. I've never said I was much of a writer. I'm just a lover of people. And a head-over-heels lover of Jesus Christ.

As I draw this long list to a conclusion, I save the deepest part of my heart for last. I am so deeply grateful to my co-laborers at Living Proof Ministries. I have no idea what I'd do without you. Don't make me find out. You are my best friends in the world.

A lump wells in my throat as I thank Amanda and Melissa, my beloved daughters. I can only imagine how hard it has been at times to have a mom who makes her life, and consequently yours, an open book. You have never been anything but supportive while I've told all manner of story on you. You are excellent young women and the most blatant proof of my life that God has redeemed the years the locusts have eaten.

Curt, my dear son-in-law, thank you for joining the madness. You are my favorite preacher.

Keith, my darling, you are my true partner in ministry and certainly in this message. Even after all we've been through, I'd choose you over and over again just to get to the point we are now. I am still so in love with you. Let's have lots of grandbabies together.

And thank You, my faithful Savior, for pulling me out of the pit and for risking Your name on me. I adore You.

Foreword

I am honored that my wife asked me to write this foreword. You'll soon understand why there is only one writer in our family. I met my wife nearly thirty years ago at a fraternity party. She was by far the most beautiful girl there. Still is. It was the start of an unlikely love affair that no one could understand. People were puzzled because we didn't seem to have anything in common.

When I was two and a half years old, my four-year-old brother, Duke, and I were caught in an explosion and trapped inside a burning garage. Quick action by my father saved my life. I literally saw my brother, Duke, burn to death.

Beth had her own trauma at an early age. We both tried to understand what had happened to us. She sought understanding by trying to find Jesus while I tried to find peace through Man's psychology.

Satan came for both of us very early. I guess he figured he could hurt more people by twisting us up than by killing us outright. What Satan meant for evil, however, God meant for good. He made the pain of our wounds so unbearable that we were willing to do anything to break out of the generational bondage that tried to hold us. You name it: alcoholism, betrayal, abandonment, depression, rage, sexual addiction, and almost anything else you can think of were our heritage. We fought hard with each other in our own version of what the

Bible calls iron sharpening iron. I hurt so badly at times that I prayed God would let me die if my pain couldn't be used for some higher good.

By now I guess you see what we had in common thirty years ago. We were both profoundly wounded with little hope of wholeness.

But God is in the hope business. He renewed our minds and set His sights on all the living generations of our families. I have witnessed God's pursuit of our nieces, nephews, brothers, and sisters for His eternal glory. We receive our salvation in a moment but we are never meant to stop there and settle for living life on the surface. As Philippians 2:12–13 says, we must "continue to work out [our] salvation . . . for it is God who works in [us] to will and to act according to his good purpose." We have to keep working things through with God until freedom and purpose come.

I am one blessed man. I love my wife. She is funny, smart, pretty, fun to be with, and she loves Jesus. She knows these Scriptures up and down, backward and forward. Most of all, I love the way the Holy Spirit and she join up to teach and inspire people to take up the sword (see Ephesians 6:17) and get back in the battle of life.

She's no phony. I can tell you she's real. A Texan can smell a varmint from a mile away. This book is rich in word and wisdom. Join with Beth and me, grab your sword, and get back in the fight. Life is worth fighting for.

—Keith Moore

INTRODUCTION

A few days ago I stood in a line for something my Bible study publisher called a "meet and greet." I had the joy of hugging at least a hundred and fifty necks of studio audience members for the Bible-study taping we'd just concluded. Laughter and happy testimonies filled the room and flooded my heart. By the time I hugged the last person, however, my mind was spinning from the more private kinds of things that had been whispered in my ear. One woman had recently lost a twenty-two-year-old daughter in a car accident. Inconceivably, another just behind her had buried a beloved three-year-old not long ago. Then I hugged a precious woman with a brightly colored scarf hiding the ravages of breast cancer that had recently metastasized to her brain. Beside her stood her sister who was doing everything she could not to give way to bitterness. A few minutes later I hugged the neck of someone battling an eating disorder. Then I embraced a pastor's wife whose husband had recently been invited out of their church. Another person slipped me a piece of paper and whispered, "Just read the note, but not right now!" The note was a request for prayer that she would be delivered from a long-term addiction.

I stared out of the window on the plane ride home and tried to take it all in. There above the clouds and turbulence, I held letters I'd been given open to God as if He could see them better in hands at high altitude. I told Him again what I'll tell you: people are hurting. He already knew. I bet you did too.

Life can be excruciating. Crushing, in fact. The sheer magnitude of our worries can press down on our heads until we unknowingly descend into a pit of despair one inch at a time. Something so horrible can happen that we conclude we'll never be okay again. We can blow it so badly we think God would just as soon we stayed under that dirt and out of His sight. But, if we're willing to let truth speak louder than our feelings, and long enough that our feelings finally agree, we can be far more than okay. We can be delivered to a place where the air is crisp, the enemy is whipped, and the view is magnificent.

The Bible teaches that there are no lost causes. No permanent pit-dwellers except those who refuse to leave. Every person can know the complete redemption of Jesus Christ, purpose for life, and fullness of joy. No, life won't ever be easy but the trade-off is a spin around Planet Earth that actually means something. I am convinced that when the last chapter of each life story is recorded in the annals of heaven, people would rather have lived out their fullness of days with purpose more than painlessness.

The words in the coming chapters fell completely fresh on me, as I pray with all my heart they will fall on you. They are not revisions of an old message. Each season of my life offers a new lesson, adds a new perspective, and the old fervor burns on and on. I suppose, as the chorus goes, "Redeeming love has been my theme and shall be till I die." God has not ceased to stir messages of deliverance in my heart from the time I took my first breath of fresh air outside the pit. An insatiable, almost maddening desire burns in my soul to see every human being live the life and fulfill the destiny Christ died and rose again to offer.

My life passion is to encourage people to come to know and love Jesus Christ through the study of His Word. My life message within that passion, however, is complete and glorious freedom. The kind only Christ can bring. I do not know why but it has never been enough for me to be free. I want you to be free too. It is not enough for me to know the thrill of God's presence. I want you to know it too. I want you to know the power of His Word that can defy every addiction, heal any affliction, and plug up every pit. I want you to know a love that is better than life. Because I have.

And I was a wreck.

I remember the first time I ever got an upgrade on a flight. I hadn't earned it with frequent flyer miles. They'd run out of room in economy and, since I was traveling alone, they told me they needed my seat and were moving me up. Throughout the flight I was so excited that I acted like a five-year-old. I kept looking at the people to my right and left and saying, "Isn't this fun? Can you believe this? Can you believe we're sitting up here?"

Strangely, they could. I was a tad much for them. Not nearly cool enough. The whole time the flight attendant served us, I fought the overwhelming desire to hop up and help her. If I thanked her once, I thanked her a thousand times. The whole cabin was worn out by the time we reached our destination. I didn't get an upgrade for a while. I think the airlines sent out a memo.

Believe me when I say I got an upgrade from the pit and I didn't earn it either. Though it's been years since I got it, I am still overwhelmed by it. I think about it every single day. A pauper to God's scandalous grace, all I know to do with the overflow is serve.

I'm writing to tell you I believe God has scheduled your flight out of a pit. You're going to need to show up for it, though. My prayer is that what follows will serve as an itinerary. Yep, you've got an offer for an upgrade right here in front of you. You really can move up and out of that pit. If you'll grant me the privilege, I'd like to be your flight attendant for a while. I've taken this trip before. It's bumpy but the destination is worth it. Thanks for having me along.

I waited patiently for the LORD;

    he turned to me and heard my cry.

He lifted me out of the slimy pit,

    out of the mud and mire;

    he set my feet on a rock

    and gave me a firm place to stand.

He put a new song in my mouth,

    a hymn of praise to our God.

    Many will see and fear

    and put their trust in the LORD.

—Psalm 40:1–3

I WAITED patiently *for the* LORD;

CHAPTER ONE

Life in the Pit

You don't have to stay there. Even if you've been there your whole life, you can call it a day. Even if you deserve the pit you live in, you're still not stuck there. Maybe you're the noble type trying to make the best of your pit. You keep wondering why you can't get satisfied there. Why you aren't mature enough to be content where you are. After all, didn't the apostle Paul tell us that we should learn to be content in any circumstance?

Has it occurred to you that maybe a pit is one place where you're not supposed to be content? Maybe you should thank God you're not. Some things weren't meant to be accepted. A pit is one of them. Quit trying to make the best of it. It's time to get out. When Christ said, "Come, follow me," inherent in His invitation to come was the equivalent invitation to leave. The laws of physics tell you that if you try to go one place without leaving another, you're in for a pretty severe stretch. And you can only do the splits so long.

Don't get me wrong. I'm not talking about picking up and leaving a physical place—although that may ultimately prove necessary. And if you're married, Lord help me, I'm certainly not talking about leaving your spouse. I'm talking about leaving a dwelling far more intimate than the place where you get your mail—I'm talking about a shadowy home of the heart, mind, and soul so close and personal that, like mud on the set of tires, we drag it along wherever our physical circumstances move us.

No matter where we go, a pit can always fit. On any path we can spin our wheels and throw mud until we dig a ditch right into the middle of an otherwise decent job or relationship. Soon our hearts sink with the dismal realization that we're no better off in our new situation. The scenery around us may have changed, but we're still living in that same old pit. We start scrambling to figure out how we're going to dump an unpleasant person or position when the real solution may be to dump that pit we dragged in. The problem is the pit can be so close we can't see it.

My man, our two dogs, and I just got home from a seven-teen-hundred-mile road trip sewing five states together like a patchwork quilt. It's something we do several times a year. For hours on end Beanie sniffs the air conditioner in search of game birds (Beanie is one of the dogs, not the man) and Sunny never quits smiling unless she needs to scratch. The glee rolls on and the miles roll by until someone gets a little cranky. I'll not name names, but God forgives the lapses and has even extended many a tender mercy by providing a timely respite from the open road. He shows us all sorts of favor, like causing espresso bars to pop up in places so remote I end up wondering later if they were really there at all. I figure they were mirages we'd never find again in a million years. But as long as the refreshment hits the spot, I don't care if it's all in my mind. I've had the best medium-dry cappuccinos in the world in places so far out that an extra shot is what you take when you missed the deer the first time.

Unfortunately, our traveling snobbery only goes as far as our coffee. When you insist on traveling cross-country with two sizable canines, you get to save your cash on motel rooms. We mostly stay in lodgings that have numbers in the names. No matter what the chain, all discount rooms are nearly identical, with angular double beds covered by the same navy-blue spreads ordered from a catalog back in '72. The stitching has long since come undone, and when you turn over in the bed your little toes get tangled in the loose threads. I sleep between Keith (that's my man) and Beanie and, from the sound of things, each has a deviated septum. I respond by turning up the air condition-ing unit which, in turn, responds by freezing up and shutting down.

A traveler at heart, I still wake up happy and start my abbreviated morning routine. The shampoo comes in a small single-serving pouch I have to open with my teeth. I spit out what gets in my mouth and quickly lather the rest of it on my head. I have a mass of hair so, understandably, I can't spare a drop. Keith ends up having to use the generic white bar soap on his hair. It tends to leave a film, but it's a small price for him to pay for my hair. Particularly small compared to what he pays for me to maintain my highlights. He can wear a baseball cap anyway.

Folks who know how much we travel sometimes ask me why we don't get an RV. The answer, in a word: the bathroom. (Or is that two words?) The small space and lack of fresh air in an RV makes the presence of a bathroom so . . . well . . . inescapable. They say you get used to it, but do I really want to? What does it mean when we no longer notice that smell? Nope, the way I see it, we were not meant to get used to some things.

Like living in a pit.

But unfortunately, we do. We can grow so accustomed to the surroundings of our pit that we wouldn't think of moving on without it.

Let's say for years you've been living in an old RV so small you can't stretch your legs or stand up straight. Visualize the clutter of too much baggage in too small a space. Imagine the unavoidable odor of that cramped lavatory. Your clothes even start to smell like it. Or is it your hair?

Now, imagine that you've been offered a brand-new home. A real one on a solid foundation with big closets and wide-open spaces. You can hardly wait to move in. Filled with anticipation, you rev up the motor of the old RV and plow it right into the new living room, taking out a wall or two on the way. Ah, finally! A new place to call home! You settle back in your RV seat, take a deep breath and poise yourself to feel something fresh. Something different.

Then it hits you: that deep breath tasted a lot like that old lavatory. You'd hoped for a change, but your soul sinks with the realization that, though you're somewhere new, everything feels and smells hauntingly familiar.

As disheartening as this realization may be, it could turn out to be the best news you've heard all year. If it wakes you up to the possibility that every situation you're in feels like a pit because you're taking your pit with you, you've just learned something you really need to know: you could quit driving that stinking RV around. This is a glorious exception to the "If the shoe fits, wear it" rule. Even if the steering wheel fits, you don't have to keep gripping it.

If you figure out you're the one driving that old RV, please understand right now that the last thing I want to do is shame you. The only reason I recognize a mobile pit dweller is because it takes one to know one. I just may have stumbled on the one thing I'm an expert on: life in the pit. When it comes to pits, I guess I've lived in every conceivable kind. I've done the tour, trading in one model for another from childhood well into adulthood. A pit was my ever present hell in times of trouble. And the only reason I've got the audacity to write this book is because I'm not there anymore. I got out because something—*Someone*—worked for me. Trust me when I tell you this: if I can get out, anybody can.

I might have kept this pit stop to myself except for something a number of people recently told me. Several months ago God threw me into His Word to perform a sort of analysis of what a *pit* is exactly. I plopped open my trusty concordance, looked up every occasion where the term was used, and went to work. There in the pages of Scripture God showed me three ways we can get into a pit and a couple of ways we can get out. The message fell so fresh on me that in the months that followed I delivered some form of it at three very different gatherings. The first was a group of four thousand women of all ages in California. The second was also a group of thousands, but this event was comprised entirely of college girls. The third was a very polished studio audience at a taping for television.

Toward the end of each message I asked the same questions. The first: "After all you've learned biblically about a pit, how many of you would say you've been in one?" In all three groups, every single hand in sight shot up into the air. Not surprising. The second question: "How many of you have gotten into various pits all three ways I spoke about?" Almost every single hand came up, mine included. I asked them to close their eyes for the last question: "How many of you would say you are in a pit right now?" To my surprise, a stunning majority of timid hands inched up—only shoulder high, just in case their neighbors were peeking.

So, what's the big surprise? If I were a betting woman, I'd have wagered all three groups contained the cream of the crop of God-seeking, Jesus-following women. Many of them have been in Bible studies for years. Scads of them are considered successful by their peers. Others look to them as the examples. As for the college girls, significant numbers of them sense God's call on their lives. Plenty are spiritual . . . and miserable.

I've come to the conclusion that vastly more people are miserable than not. Far more feel defeated than victorious. If pressed, tens of thousands would confess that "it" doesn't work as well as they'd hoped. Masses of believers are totally bewildered—if not in outright despair. Yep, poker faces aside, they're in a pit. Not without cause, but absolutely, across the board, unnecessarily. I've also come to the conclusion that some pits are just decorated to look prettier than others. Don't let anybody kid you, though. A pit is a pit.

That's the trouble. Too often we don't recognize a pit when we're in one. So why would we think we need to get out? One reason some of you nicer folks are in a pit without realizing it is because you mistakenly characterize pits only in terms of sin. In our Christian subculture, we think a pit of sin is the only kind there is. But as we perform a biblical analysis of a pit, we're going to have to think much broader than that. We need a way to identify pits and know when we're in them. So here goes: you can know you're in a pit when . . .

You feel stuck. Isaiah 42:22 says that a pit is a place where you feel trapped. You tend to feel your only options are to misbehave (i.e., have a kicking and screaming fit, hoping your flailing can help you escape) or submit (i.e., consider you made your own bed and decide to die in it). Psalm 40 adds to the characteristics of a pit words like "slimy," "muddy," "miry." Together these words tell us one critical thing about a pit: you can't get yourself out.

Been there in more ways than one. Keith waited only a few months into our marriage before trying to turn his animal-rights wife into a hunter. He thought it wisest to start with creatures that were furless. Feathers, he reasoned, would make the hunt seem less personal. He dressed me for my first and only goose hunt in the last pair of rubber boots under a size 12 at the army surplus. He realized at the checkout that they were both right feet, but since they were a bit large he thought they'd work just fine. Smiling ear to ear like he'd bagged a ten-point buck, Keith plopped those black monsters right in front of me. I looked down at the tips of two boots making the same turn then stared at him for the longest. I told him that wherever we were going, I hoped it was to the right.

Dawn was unmerciful. I found myself trudging behind him way too early on a cold morning in a flooded rice field outside of Houston. Every third step I took, one of my right feet got stuck in the mud until finally one of them stuck so deeply that, for the life of me, I couldn't get myself out.

"Pull, Baby! Pull!" Keith cheered.

"I'm trying!" I yelled. "They won't come up!"

Every second I stood there, I sunk another inch. When the oozing mud began toppling into my boots, I finally did what any self-respecting woman would do: I bawled. Exasperated, Keith turned around and started back for me. He was muttering something under his breath that I couldn't exactly make out, but I was pretty sure somebody needed to wash his mouth out. I was also pretty sure he was in no mood for it to be me. He tugged and tugged until he pulled my stocking feet right out of my boots. We hiked back to the car early that day, birdless, bootless, and with me on his back. It wasn't the last time.

Sinking inch by inch. That's what happens in a pit. Jeremiah knew the feeling and, mind you, he hadn't even sinned his way into it. Jeremiah 38:6 describes his pit as a place of sinking down. Imagine how much worse it was with sandals. No matter what's on your feet, you can take this fact to the spiritual bank: a pit only gets deeper. Low ground always sinks. There's no living at maintenance level in a pit.

You'd think enough has already been said about the irony of Christians and substandard living . . . even from my own loud mouth and scrawling pen. I don't know why, but it drives me nuts that people stay in bad places when they don't have to. That's a big part of what makes a pit a pit. Feeling stuck.

I guess it drives me nuts to see them living in those pits because I've been there. I was stuck quite a while myself before I realized I didn't have to stay there. And now that I'm no longer stuck, I want everybody else out of that trap.

You can't stand up. In Psalm 69:2, David cried out, "I sink in deep mire, where there is no standing" (NKJV). If you're not already convinced, it's time you accepted the biblical fact that your soul has a very real enemy, and he is not flesh and blood. We can't keep on ignoring someone who is systematically trying to destroy our lives. The passivity has got to go. Ephesians 6:11 implores us, "Take your stand against the devil's schemes." *Your* stand. No one can stand indefinitely for you. If you and I are going to be victorious people, we've got to stand with our own two feet on solid ground. Ephesians 6:13 exhorts, "Stand your ground, and after you have done everything, to stand."

One way you can know you're in a pit is that you feel ineffective and utterly powerless against attack. You can't stand up to assaults, trials, or temptations because your feet are in the mud and mire. You experience what the psalmist experienced and what I certainly experienced—you're in a place "where there is no standing." That's why the testimony of the person rescued from the pit paints this vivid picture of an all-new venue: "He set my feet upon a rock and gave me a firm place to stand" (Psalm 40:2b).

I beg you to see that your enemy has a tremendous investment not only in digging and camouflaging a pit in your pathway but also, should you tumble down, in convincing you to stay there after you fall in. He knows that in his pit you will feel powerless to stand up against him. There you are vulnerable to him and out of his way.

To the ancient Hebrew, a pit was a literal or figurative reference to the grave—to its threat—or to an abyss so deep the dweller within it felt like the living dead. Been there? Me too. Drawing from the figurative application, we'll define *pit* this way: a pit is an early grave that Satan digs for you in hopes he can bury you alive. Should you fall into it, make no mistake; he cannot make you stay. Ironically, neither will God make you leave. Like it or not, some things are simply up to us.

You've lost vision. Unlike that rank old RV, pits have no windows. Scripture paints them as places of darkness. I'm not talking about demonic darkness, although if we go deep enough and stay long enough, we will certainly encounter the darkness of utter evil. I'm talking about something more basic than that. I'm referring to the kind of darkness that simply impairs our vision. A pit is so poorly lit we can no longer see things that may have once been obvious to us. That's another reason we often stay in a pit. Without windows we're convinced we have nowhere else to go. Yes, we can always look up—goodness knows that's the only opening we have—but we're often too focused on our sinking feet to crane our necks to the blinding sky. We become what the Bible calls stiff necked. The close confinement of a pit exhausts us with the endless echo of self-absorption. Visibility extends no further than six inches from our noses. We can't see out, so we turn our sights in. After a while, nearsightedness breeds hopelessness. We feel too buried in our present state to feel passionate about a promised future.

Created in the image of God, we are meant to brim over with creativity. Yes, that means you. Don't tell me you're not the creative type. I'm not talking right-brain-versus left-brain drivel. I'm not talking about accountant types versus actor types. All image-bearers of God were intended to overflow with effervescent life, stirring and spilling with God-given vision. That's partly what the apostle Paul was talking about when he prayed that the eyes of our hearts would be enlightened in order that we might know the hope to which Christ has called us (see Ephesians 1:18). The Amplified Bible calls it "having the eyes of your heart flooded with light." That's what you miss in the pit.

Our imaginations were fashioned like wicks to be ignited by the fire of fresh revelation, dripping with wax that God can imprint with His endless signatures. He writes in fonts and shades we've yet to see, telling us who He is and what He's capable of doing. In the light of God's face shining upon us, we also glimpse reflections of our true selves. We were meant to see ourselves as part of something so much bigger than we are. Something vital. Something incredibly thrilling. But the eyes of some of us have adjusted to the darkness of the pit surrounding us. We've forgotten what we used to see or shrugged off those early divine encounters as something we must have made up when we were less mature, just as Susan Pevensie did after returning from Narnia. In the final Narnia story, *The Last Battle*, C. S. Lewis tells us that Susan, who in *The Lion, the Witch and the Wardrobe* witnessed the death and resurrection of the godlike lion Aslan, looked back on her times in Narnia as "funny games we used to play as children." She ultimately came to the conclusion that the heavenly land of her childhood experience was nothing more than a childish fantasy because she was "a jolly sight too keen on being grownup."

Dim vision ages us rapidly, and we lose the childlikeness that once made us feel like real princes and princesses in a kingdom. We can be young and yet feel old. Heavy laden. Burdened. In a pit where vision is lost and dreams are foolishness.

Through the pages to come, some of you will recognize your pits. For most of you awareness won't come because you suddenly see how bad you are, but rather because you will wake up to how bored you are. The lack of light and fresh air has lulled some of us to sleep. Getting out begins with waking up. *And* (this may be the hardest part) with being willing to feel again.

In Psalm 40:2 David exclaimed,

> He lifted me out of the slimy pit,
>> out of the mud and mire;
>
> he set my feet on a rock
>> and gave me a firm place to stand.

According to Psalm 27:6, high upon that very rock "my head will be exalted above the enemies who surround me." See what Satan has to lose when you get out of your pit? Not only are wonder, hope, and vision natural when our feet are set upon a rock, but so is our vantage point from which we can see the enemy's activity around us. (Incidentally, there's no one on earth Satan would rather see in a pit than someone with godly vision. Just ask Joseph.)

There you have it. We don't have to be in a stronghold of sin to be in a pit. We just have to feel stuck, feel we can't stand up to our enemy, and feel like we've lost our vision. That's all it takes to constitute a pit. Ever been in one? Are you in one now? Is somebody you love in one? How in the world does a person get into these pits? More important, how does one get out? These are the questions we will answer in the rest of this book.

HE TURNED TO ME

and *heard* MY CRY.

CHAPTER TWO

When You're Thrown Into a Pit

Yow can get thrown in. That's right, without doing one thing to deserve it and without wallowing your way into it. I'm not talking about a pit of sin here. This one's a pit of innocence—the kind a lot of believers don't realize exists. You can get thrown right into the miry deep before you know what hit you. Or worse yet, before you know *who* hit you. In fact, those were the very circumstances surrounding the first pit ever mentioned in Scripture. Genesis 37:23–25 records the details:

> When Joseph came to his brothers, they stripped off his robe, the robe of many colors that he had on. Then they took him and threw him into the pit. The pit was empty; there was no water in it. Then they sat down to eat a meal. (HCSB)

In a fit of jealous rage set up by their father's partiality, the older sons of Jacob threw their seventeen-year-old little brother, Joseph, into a cistern with the intention of leaving him for dead. Let that sink in a second. Perhaps you've read the story so many times the brothers' actions no longer seem like a big deal. After all, things turned out okay, right?

I sat across the table from a gifted woman of God not long ago who told me that when she was little her father put her out of the car on a country road because she was crying. He then proceeded to drive off. He came back and got her a little later, his feathers puffed up like a rooster, hoping she'd learned a lesson. She learned a lesson all right: she learned she couldn't trust her father.

In spite of all I've seen and heard, when she told me this story it was all I could do to keep my chin off the floor. I was utterly horrified. Since this woman has been greatly used of God, you might reason that things turned out okay for her too. But I assure you, the price of her redemption was sky high. Every day she must consciously make the choice to believe her godly husband is not going to drop her off somewhere and never come back. Never minimize the choice someone like her makes daily to dig her heels securely in the rock and not slip back in that familiar pit that continually beckons, "Come home! Come home!"

The New King James Version words Psalm 40:2 this way: "[God] also brought me up out of a horrible pit." Yep, that says it. Some pits are just plain horrible. And when we sit across from someone bearing witness to one of these, horror can be an appropriate first response. I hope never to reach the point where I cease to cry over some of the stories I hear. Every story you hear, every account you read, happens to real, live flesh and blood that bruises, gushes, and scars. So many of the people surrounding us have suffered horrifically in a pit they did not dig for themselves. Often they first need the simple validation of someone saying to them, "That is *horrible*. I am so sorry that I hardly know what to say." Then, when trust is earned and the time is right, we can testify to our hope.

The ways we can get thrown into a pit are as varied as the footprints planted in them:

- Like my young friends, Cara, Christen, and Amanda, who watched a drunk teenager drive her car off the road, into the yard, and over their mother, you can be thrown into a pit by sudden tragedy.
- Like one precious woman in Bible study who was stabbed repeatedly by a boyfriend she tried to break up with, you can be thrown into the pit by a violent crime.
- Like my family of origin, you can be thrown into a pit by a loved one suffering from mental illness. I cannot adequately voice the fear that can be incited by someone with serious bouts of irrational thinking.
- Also like my family, you can be thrown into a pit by an alcoholic leaving a deep path of destruction

too wide to avoid. I cast no condemnation on this loved one. There but for the grace of God should have gone I.

- Like my friend Sara, you can be thrown into a pit by your spouse's declaration that, after twenty years of marriage, he's in love with someone else, and he's leaving.

- Like Sara's children, you can be thrown into a pit by a parent who suddenly abandons the home. If you're fortunate, you're still told how much you are loved, but somehow all you can feel is how you've been left.

- Like Eric, a brother in Christ, you can be thrown into a pit by a heartless woman who says you've bored her to tears and she's going to have some fun without you.

- Like my friend Shawn and staggering numbers of others, you can be thrown into the pit by a life-threatening disease. Even imminent death.

- Like Jim and Connie, you can be thrown into a pit by the birth of a severely handicapped child who may never recognize your face but will probably outlive you.

- Like Charles and Gayle, you can be thrown into a pit by a house fire that happened in one brief window of opportunity when you had no insurance.

- Like numerous members of my church in Houston, you can be thrown into a pit by traumatic financial loss when a company like Enron comes tumbling down.

- Like eight-year-old Jay and twelve-year-old Angela, you can be thrown into a pit when your successful father goes to prison for corporate crimes.

- Or, like so many children standing in the same line with Melissa and me as we waited to see a loved one who was doing time in jail, you can be thrown into a pit by a crackhead parent who rarely sobers up enough to care. Make no mistake. A pit offers ready residence to the rich and poor alike. Pain couldn't care less about your social status. All bleed when they're cut ... unless they're finally bled out.

- Like me, you can be thrown into a pit by a close relative selfish and sick enough to molest you when you were a child.

- Like me, you can be thrown into a pit by the rejection of someone you wanted and felt you needed so desperately to love you.

- Like my husband, Keith, you can be thrown into the pit by the sudden death of a sibling while you were playing together and, like him, end up wishing it had been you.

Also like my husband, you can be thrown into a pit when you lose yet another sibling and you're left to wonder why some families suffer so much more than others. Life is danged unfair.

Give this one a little extra reverence with me: Like Mary, Sue, Ginny, Heather, Buddy, Randy, and so many others with real names and real pain, you can be thrown into a pit by the death of a beloved, irreplaceable child.

Like you . . . ?

These examples are no more fun for me to write than they are for you to read. But I don't know how we're ever going to get out of a pit we refuse to recognize or talk about. Mind you, we could experience blows like these without necessarily descending into the pit, but the chances of enduring such horrors without entering the darkness for at least a little while are about as good as Joseph gripping the edges of that cistern and resisting the shove of his brothers. The downward force of some circumstances can be almost too much to resist.

Many of us found ourselves in a pit long before we reached Joseph's age of seventeen. To be completely candid with you, I don't even remember life before the pit. I demonstrated behavioral patterns of a victim of abuse long before I went to kindergarten. Frequent pit-visiting has a way of turning into pit-living. The earlier we enter the pit or the longer we stay, the

28

more it feels like home. We start hanging our pictures on the wall, tidying up the place, and making ourselves comfortable. We invite others over to visit us in the pit, and sometimes they feel sufficiently enough at home to unpack their bags. If we're cool enough, we may even move a Pottery Barn couch and Williams Sonoma kitchenware right into the middle of it. But as soon as the rain comes, it all gets soiled. That's the trouble. Every pit has a dirt floor.

Of all three ways to get into a pit, getting thrown in—not by *something* but by *someone*—can be the most complicated to deal with emotionally and spiritually. I'll give you a few reasons why. For starters, when someone throws us in, we've obviously got someone to blame. *It's all their fault.* Talk about a scenario with the capacity to eat us alive! Often when someone else puts us in a pit, we know in the depths of our heart that it wasn't his or her intention. Take, for instance, a family member with mental illness, or a parent who neglects her healthy children because she can't help focusing most of her attention on one desperately handicapped child. As much as pain can skew our thinking, motives and intentions still mean a great deal to us, and knowing that someone never meant to hurt us can lift us considerably in our ascent from the pit. The emotions involved are still complicated, but not nearly as much as they could be had the hurt been intentional.

You want to talk complications? Okay, how about times when you've been thrown into the pit by someone else's sin, and that someone happens to be a family member? Or a loved one who was supposed to love you back? Getting over the trauma would have been hard enough had Joseph been thrown into the pit by strangers who picked him randomly. Instead, his own flesh and blood did it . . . and they meant to. Been there? Me too.

All right, let's twist that rag a little tighter. Look once again at the excerpt from the Genesis account that I quoted toward the beginning of this chapter. I purposely included that insidious last line that tells how Joseph's brothers, after throwing him into the pit, "then . . . sat down to eat a meal." Ponder that a moment. They'd just thrown their own kicking and screaming sibling into a deep hole, yet they apparently weren't sick to their stomachs. They didn't run for their lives. They sat right there, pulled out their PB&Js and ate lunch. Infuriating, isn't it? Genesis 42:21 describes what was emanating from the pit while the brothers had their picnic. The Amplified Bible says it best: "We saw the distress and anguish of his soul when he begged us [to let him go], and we would not hear."

What about times when a person has been used by the enemy to throw us into a pit, and he or she remains close by, lives on as if nothing has ever happened (eating, working, playing, going to church, etc.), sees our distress and anguish, but *will not hear* us? Maybe even despises us for our weakness. Ah, now that's complicated. I know from experience. What's even more tragic is the humiliating lengths we'll go to in order to make someone hear us, and all we end up doing is digging our pits deeper. How often have I made a fool of myself just trying to get someone who hurt me to hear me?

Beloved, I hate to have to bring up this word, but I just don't have a choice. It's the last word any of us want to hear echoing back and forth in a pit we've been thrown into. You already know what this word is, and you're probably sick of hearing it. But we don't want to be like those who hold something against others because they "would not hear," do we? Then we've got to open our ears and hear that difficult word again: *forgive*. It's a tough thing to do, but we've got to forgive, even—no, *especially*—those who don't care to be forgiven.

Through the infused power of His own Spirit, forgive like Christ forgave when He said, "Father, forgive them, for they do not know what they are doing." Translation: "They don't have a clue." Whoever threw you into the pit doesn't have any idea how much it hurt you. I'm not sure they would get it even if you told them in detail upon detail. No, they don't have a clue how much it affected your decisions and relationships. Humbly, but very specifically, forgive them not only for their destructive actions, but also for their *ignorance*. You have no other choice if you want out of that pit.

I know you've heard all this a thousand times, but this could be the day it sinks in, dear one. This could be the day of your deliverance. You think you can't do it? I felt the same way. I heard over and over how I'd have to forgive, but I just folded my arms over my chest in a huff and refused to do anything about it. You see, I started out in a pit of innocence, but through the years my bitterness rearranged the furniture until it was nothing more than a well-camouflaged pit of sin. I thought forgiving my pit-throwers would make what happened all right. But, to be sure, it didn't. Still isn't. What I didn't understand about forgiveness was that it would make *me* all right. One day I finally began getting the message, and I'm praying right now that this is that day for you.

I want to tell you a few things that have helped me in my ascent out of the pit of unforgiveness. God changed the way I looked at the entire situation when I began to see that my grudge against people who hurt me only strengthened the grip of my bondage to them. The Greek word translated "nursed a grudge against" in Mark 6:19 means "to hold on, endure . . . Metaphorically, to be held in or by anything; to be entangled in something, be enmeshed, to be subject to."[1] How do you like that? Our grudges only work to further entangle and enmesh us with the persons we won't forgive. How ironic! When we won't forgive, the people we often want to be around least because they've hurt us so badly are the very people we take with us emotionally everywhere we go. Get this: we are "subject to" them through our own unforgiveness. Do you want to be subject to someone who has hurt you terribly? Neither do I.

I'll tell you something else that helped me greatly. Most people may think of forgiveness as spineless passivity, but I began to look at it as tremendous empowerment. I don't want to be graphic, but I suppose you can imagine that abuse or rape victims suffer long and hard—whether emotionally or physically—over the passivity forced upon them at the time of the crime. Somehow the thought of having to forgive only made me feel more abused, as if I was forced to be passive to the perpetrator once again.

My breakthrough came when I realized that nothing took more divine power than forgiveness, and therefore nothing was more powerful than forgiving. You will never use your own volition—the force of your will—more dramatically than when you agree with God to start forgiving. Forgiveness is not about feeling. It's about *willing*. No stronger force exists. Forgiveness was the force that kept Christ, by His own submission, nailed to that cross. He could have taken Himself down in a split second. He could have called upon every archangel in the heavens, armed and ready. Had He said the word, the seas would have swallowed the earth in one gulp.

Forgiveness is not passivity, dear one. It is power. It is the ability to withstand the pressing, quaking gates of hell. Take this power and wield it. It's your right as a child of God. In the power of Jesus, first you will it and soon you'll feel it. Start today. Confirm it tomorrow. And keep confirming it by faith as the will of God for you in Christ Jesus until you walk it by sight. You don't have to have a background like mine to resist passivity in your response to wrongdoing. You can resist it just as readily when responding to abandonment by a spouse or the betrayal of a friend.

The Christian experience teems with so many paradoxes. Among them is the fact that it takes far more strength and personal fortitude to fall on our knees and submit to God than to stand and fight our endless battles for significance. Don't let anyone make you think that forgiveness is a covenant with weakness. Nothing demands more elbow grease than thrusting your arms forward and giving God the solitary right to vengeance.

So far we've talked about how we tend to blame people we feel were used by Satan to throw us into a pit. But there can be a couple of other scenarios that make blame equally irresistible. The Book of Job suggests them both. It's not coincidental that Job refers to a pit numerous times, because nothing invites us to draw near to an early grave like suffering and loss. Simply put, suffering and loss can make us wish we were dead. And since Satan wishes the same thing—he was, after all, a "murderer from the beginning"—his job is to keep us in that morbid mindset. In such anguish of soul, our human natures thrash and grasp about for someone to blame when things go wrong.

Job's friends tried to get him to blame himself. Haven't most of us been there and felt the sickening urge toward self-blame? *It's all my fault.* Not at the insistence of our friends, perhaps. If you're like me, it was more often at the insistence of your own secret self-loathing. One reason Satan continues his self-employment as the accuser (see Revelation 12:10) is because the job is so easy and so rewarding. He knows that even when we're innocent of any reason for being in a pit, we are well aware that we are far from innocent in other things. He plays mind games with our consciences so that for the life of us, we can't seem to distinguish between those areas where we are guilty and those where we are innocent.

For instance, a woman who has been raped may be tormented by memories of times when she wasn't innocent in physical relationships in the past. She now listens to the accuser, loses her ability to discriminate, and decides she must have asked to be raped. *Wrong.*

Got the picture? Let's snap a few more. A man abandoned by his wife can decide he deserved to be left because he worked too hard. Nope. Maybe he deserved some serious confrontations. Maybe he deserved to be dragged into counseling. But did he deserve a divorce?

Their kids take on guilt because they are certain that what really caused the breakup was the fighting between themselves. They knew they should have quit. And they should have cleaned up their rooms. Now look what they've caused.

Hand them all a shovel.

Behold the added havoc the enemy can wreak when he suggests ever so cleverly that you dug that pit, it fits you, and you'd better crawl in it. Listen carefully: you can be in a pit innocently even if you haven't always been innocent. Give yourself a break. No one but the smallest child has *always* been innocent. Not even Joseph. If you ask me, that boy was a brat. Are you telling me a seventeen-year-old doesn't have the sense to know when his bragging has every man's robe in the house tied in a square knot? Genesis 37:4 says his brothers couldn't even say a kind word to him. Did Joseph somehow miss that subliminal message? And, for crying out loud, was it absolutely necessary for him to wear that galling multicolored coat when he went to check on his brothers? I mean, the boy needed to get a clue.

But did he deserve to be thrown into a pit? I don't think so.

So, maybe the question is not, "Have you done *anything* wrong?" Maybe the better question is, "Have you done the wrong that fits the pit?" If you have, well, so have I, and we'll deal with that in the next few chapters. If you haven't, you're in a pit of innocence . . . whether or not you're unarguably innocent in every other area of your life.

To his enormous credit, my husband, Keith, has had enough counseling to start his own practice. He needn't go out looking for business, however, because our own family has enough issues to keep him busy until he sees Jesus. We continually get free advice from him. Good advice, as a matter of fact, and we're usually glad to get it. Usually. At the very least it makes us laugh and always makes us feel at home. It's just so . . . him.

To his wife, who has a hard time letting go of things, Keith constantly says, "Lizabeth, learning to say good-bye is a necessary life skill." To Melissa, who is working herself half to death in grad school, he chides, "B's, child. I want to see B's on your report cards. Dump your A-plus perfectionism and give me some B's." To Amanda, our tender-hearted eldest who takes too much responsibility for things she can't help, he continually says, "False guilt, child. That's your false guilt rearing up its head again!" He knows about false guilt. He's never been able to shake the feeling that he should have done something to save his four-year-old brother when they were in that house fire together. He was two years old at the time.

Satan is a master at using our own insecurity against us. He knows that deep in our hearts we're so fragile and injured by life that his faintest whisper will talk us into feeling guilty even when we're not. Satan knows the hardest person for us to forgive will always be ourself. Most people never do forgive themselves. I love the way Greg Paul describes us in *God in the Alley*: "We are alike in many ways more fundamental than

a few self-destructive habits. We are broken, fatally flawed—
and immeasurably precious, made in God's image."[2] We've got
some problems all right, but problems by themselves don't dig
pits. They just offer shovels. We provide the sweat.

We've got one other place to go before we can finish this chapter: *It's all God's fault.* It's probably the most complicated place
of all, but if we really want out of our pit, it's unavoidable.
What do we do when we feel God is to blame for the pit we're
in? Like when we've lost a loved one or lost our health? From
all the free counsel Job was getting, he could either follow his
friends' advice and blame himself, or he could follow his wife's
advice (and perhaps his own gut) and blame God. The problem with blaming God is that it charges Him with wrongdoing. Thankfully, "He knows how we are formed, he remembers
that we are dust" (Psalm 103:14). In other words, He understands us and He takes into account our limitations.

We, on the other hand, are totally incapable of understanding His ways at times. Yet in His tender mercy, God
lets us ask the same nagging question that Abraham posed:
"Will not the Judge of all the earth do right?" Maybe we ask it
using different words, such as, "Can we really be sure that God
always has our best interests at heart?" Or maybe we just say it
silently, letting our distancing hearts speak for themselves.

If we're willing to stay close enough and watch long
enough, we will discover that the answer to the question is

emphatically *yes*. The Judge of all the earth will do right. He is complete perfection. All wise. Only good. Satan has no more effective weapon in his arsenal than to make us question— not so much whether God exists, but whether God is really good. He knows God alone possesses the power and passion for us to be restored after nearly being shredded in life's killing fields. For Satan to talk us into distrusting God and distancing ourselves from Him is to keep us broken, ineffective, and frankly, out of his hair. Life offers no few invitations to fall into this kind of distrust.

I have a darling twelve-year-old friend at my church named Kendall. I have known Kendall all her life and prayed for her from the time the doctor first discovered her Down's syndrome. She has mainstreamed in sports as well as in school. I was told the first time she ran a base in softball and the first time she finished every lap at her swim meet. She and I like to wear our black boots to church on the same days. I am crazy about her.

Characteristically active, talkative, and cheerful, a few months ago Kendall became dramatically lethargic and increasingly pale. The dust hadn't settled before her parents had her in a flurry of medical tests. We were all astounded when the tests proved positive for leukemia. No, not just astounded. Horrified. In the privacy of my own safe and sound relationship with God, the news sent me whirling. Didn't she have enough to deal with? Didn't her family? Hadn't she been such a trouper? Why her? Why not me? And if my emotions whirled at Kendall's bad news, can you imagine what her family felt? (Even now, I can hardly see to write for the tears in my eyes.)

Soon after Kendall was diagnosed, I had to have some medical tests of my own. She and I text-messaged one another on cell phones from our different hospitals. She prayed for me; I prayed for her. The guilt threatened to overwhelm me when my tests came out clear after hers didn't. Maybe she'd just out-prayed me.

In God's grace and patience, He let me whirl and land feet first upon Zephaniah 3:5: "The Lord within her is righteous. He does no wrong... every new day he does not fail." The verse describes Jerusalem, but I believe God used it in that moment to speak to me about Kendall, His precious child who openly, confidently calls His Son Savior.

I know that Kendall belongs to Jesus. I don't just believe she's safe, as we sometimes say of the forever childlike. To use good old Baptist terminology, Kendall is as saved as Billy Graham. The simplicity of the gospel made perfect sense to her, and she professed her faith in Christ. So, to me, the Zephaniah Scripture fit. The Lord is within her through His Holy Spirit. And He is righteous. And He does no wrong.

I drank those words like tonic as I sat before the God I love—and trust—and wept. My feelings were hurt. Not because God was wrong but because my feelings are at times such poor reflections of truth. Right there in His presence I recounted what I knew to be true, and before long it changed what I felt. No, I can't explain how the whole goodness-of-God, suffering-of-man thing works, but I know that God cannot—does not—wrong His children. He can't. Inconceivably holy, God cannot sin. He is unapproachable Light, and He has no dark side.

At the end of the Book of Job, its protagonist didn't have his original questions answered either, but this he knew: his God was huge, his God was wise, and his God would redeem. Blaming God as a means of charging Him with wrongdoing will only dig us into a deeper pit. However, holding God ultimately responsible in the healthy way, as His Word suggests, will be our ticket out.

Stick with me here. I know I've just made a statement that I need to unpack for you, and I'm about to do that. How we react to our remaining discussion in this chapter will determine whether we stay in or get out of that pit we've been thrown into.

Think back on Joseph, our first scriptural example of a pit-dweller and one who did not dig his way into it. He had plenty of people to blame and was completely justified in doing it. A grudge, however, would only have kept his feet buried in the bottom of his pit. We may think we're jabbing our finger in the guilty one's chest when in reality we're jabbing more holes in our pit walls and throwing that much more dirt on our feet.

Somewhere along the way, Joseph decided not only to look up but also to point up. His decision to view God as entirely sovereign and ultimately responsible was not the death of him. It was the life of him. Why? Because he knew God could only be good and do right. The words Joseph spoke over his guilty brothers have been medicine to many sick souls who were willing to swallow them whole: "You intended to harm me, but God intended it for good to accomplish what is now being done, the saving of many lives" (Genesis 50:20).

Take a good look at that word *intended*. It comes from the same Hebrew word translated "think" in Jeremiah 29:11: "For I know the thoughts that I think toward you, says the LORD, thoughts of peace and not of evil, to give you a future and a hope" (NKJV). God thinks of His children continually. And when God thinks of His children, He only thinks in terms of what can be used toward our good, toward His plan for us, and toward the future. His intentions can only be pure. Right. Full of hope. Promoting peace. Listen carefully. God did not haphazardly or accidentally let Joseph's brothers throw him in the pit. He had already thought it out in advance. Considered it. Weighed it. Checked it against the plumb line of the plan. He had looked at the good it could ultimately accomplish, the lives that could be helped and even saved. Then, and only then, in His sovereign purpose did He permit such harm to come to His beloved child. Had the incident not possessed glorious purpose, God would have disarmed it.

Beloved, I don't just know this for a biblical fact; I know it for a personal fact. I live it every single day. Can you think of anything more evil than child abuse? Anything at all? When I was a little girl, God already knew the plans He had for me . . . just like He knew the plans He had for you. In His sovereignty, He allowed a series of wrongs to come to me that had mammoth effects on my life. For many years, I reaped a whirlwind of negative consequences and added insult to injury by piling all manner of sin onto my victimization. Then one day, at the bottom of my pit, I raised my weary head and dirty, tear-streaked face to the sky. And redemption drew nigh. God knew the plans He had for me. Plans to prosper me and not to harm me. Plans to give me a hope and a future. I have lived long enough to see Him accomplish everything His Word says He will. Long enough to see beauty exceed the ashes and divine pleasure exceed the pain.

Dear one, whether or not I say a word about my past, God uses it every single day without fail in my ministry. In friendship. In motherhood. In marriage. He does the same for Keith. Perhaps the only thing worse than child abuse is the death of a child. In two separate incidents Keith lost both his older brother and his younger sister. Day before yesterday he spent an hour on the phone with a friend who'd lost her young adult brother in a freak car accident. He prayed for her and told her how he'd made it through the pain. He's done it a thousand times. Keith's past doesn't just come in handy every now and then; he uses it every day, whether or not the stories ever come out of his mouth. It's part of who he is. And my past is part of who I am. Part of who God is making me.

Keith and I have been through so much—much more than we share with others—that every now and then the memories or regrets get one of us down. Last week Keith had one of those moments. We'd been discussing loved ones and their personality types. Were they sanguine, choleric, melancholy, or phlegmatic, or blends of both? He grew very serious and said, "What do you think I would have been like? You know, if all that hadn't happened. If Duke hadn't died. If my family hadn't had all those problems. If I hadn't been so messed up and turned to so much sin. What do you think I might have been like?"

I could tell Keith was lamenting the potential he might have had if life had not tailspun him in a different direction. I believe the words that came out of my mouth were from God and not from me, because I wasn't smart enough or swift enough to think of them that fast. "Honey," I responded. "You're a much neater person *healed* than you would have been well."

Oh, beloved, you keep thinking about how things might have been had *that* not happened. Would you be willing to hear those same words I spoke to Keith? You have the capacity to be a ten times neater person healed than you would have been just plain well. Your wealth of experience makes you rich. Spend it on hurt people. They need it so badly. If God can use childhood abuse and family tragedy, He can use anything. You don't have to be in full-time ministry for Him to accomplish the kind of redemption I described above. People in your workplace and your neighborhood are dying for hope. Dying to know there's a future. Dying to know there's a God . . . and that He's for them, not against them.

There's no telling what kind of bludgeon the enemy wanted to use against you and against me, but in each of our lives God has only allowed what He knew after much thought and deliberation could be used for good, for the helping— even saving—of many lives. Should you be willing to leave a legacy of faith, some of those lives you help will grace this earth after you're gone. Lives needing the kind of help you can give are surrounding you right now. Each one of them is worth the work.

God has given Keith and me the funniest daughters. They are as different as night and day, but each is as clever as the other. Last year Melissa was home for a few months between the end of college and the beginning of graduate school. (We loved having her back upstairs where she belonged, I might add.) Maybe it's really kind of ridiculous that I never put alarm clocks in the girls' rooms when they were growing up.

As sappy as this sounds, I wanted to wake them up myself. I wanted them to hear the voice of someone who loved them first thing in the morning.

Well, Melissa had been away to college for the most part of four years, but as any parent of adult children will tell you, they often lapse into their old patterns the second they slip back under their childhood covers. She had to go somewhere the next morning and asked me if I'd awaken her "like you used to, Mom." Yes, of course I would. And I did. The first time. The second time . . . The sixth time. The seventh time. She refused to get up. I finally raised my voice at her, and she responded, "Mom, get over here!" She threw back the covers of her bed, patted the fitted sheet, and said, "Lie down, Mom. Right here."

I balked. After all, her bed was a water bed with a frame all the way down on the floor and, frankly, I didn't want to expend the energy on the long descent followed by the clutching, grasping, and twisting it would take to extract myself from the pitching waves. As stubborn as an ox, she pestered me until I sat down on the bed. "No, Mom! Lie all the way down." I did. "Get under the covers." I did. "Pull the covers up." I did. "Fluff your pillow up right under your head." I did. "Feel that bed, Mom." I did. Oh, man, it felt good. Lying by my side in exactly the same posture, she looked over at me and quipped, "Now, would you want to get up if you were me?"

I've thought about that moment a thousand times. Life is hard. Most of us have reasons to lie down on life and never get up. You've been through your stuff; I've been through mine. In one way or another, at one time or another, by one person or another, each of us has been thrown into a pit. Most of us can rationalize staying angry, bitter, or fearful and insecure for the rest of our lives. Most of us can talk others into not blaming us for being in our pit. We think we want people to lie down next to us, feel what we feel, and give us permission to stay there. But if they do, they help talk us into making ourselves at home in the early grave Satan dug for us. They agree to our living death.

Christ got down next to us in the grave, stayed the better part of three days, and then got up . . . so we'd have permission to get up too. And start living life.

Beloved, let this one sink in deeply: if God allowed you to be thrown into a pit, you weren't picked on; you were picked out. God entrusted that suffering to you because He has faith in you. Live up to it. All the way up.

HE LIFTED ME

out of the slimy

ME

slimy

PIT,

CHAPTER THREE

When You Slip Into a Pit

You can slip in. That's the second way you can find yourself in a pit. Unlike the pit we get thrown into, we put ourselves into this one. But here's the catch: we didn't mean to. We just weren't watching where we were going. We got a little distracted, taken in by the new sights. The path didn't seem bad; it just seemed new. Exhilarating. We thought we were still okay, but the next thing we knew we were in a hole, our feet ankle deep in mud. The cell phone was dead, and suddenly we didn't have a clue what to do.

Yes, you got into this pit yourself, but it certainly wasn't planned. It wasn't what you wanted. In fact, falling into a pit may never have entered your mind. You certainly didn't mean for things to turn out the way they did. You didn't see it coming, but now you're in a hole.

You'd give anything if someone else had thrown you in, because you hate being the one to blame. In fact, at first you tried to think it was somebody else's fault. Anybody else's fault. But then you spent enough time in that pit for the noon sun to peak straight over your head, shedding the first direct light you'd seen there. With eyes squinting and a hand cupped on your brow, you looked up to see the marks of two suspiciously familiar heels leaving twin ruts all the way from the mouth of the pit to the bottom where you're standing now. You glance at the back of your shoes and, sure enough, they're caked with mud. That sick feeling in your stomach tells you—no matter who else was involved—nobody pushed you into this pit. You got yourself into this one. And you're not even sure how.

Right about now I wish we were sitting across from one another at the IHOP sharing stories. I'd get lemon crepes with a side of ham, and you could get the country omelet like Keith if you want to make me feel at home. But we'd hold off on ordering the coffee. It tends to be weak there, and there's a Starbucks next door. Once at Starbucks, we'd talk till lunch, then we'd transfer our conversation to a nearby hole in the wall that serves the best cheese enchiladas in Houston. I bet you could widen my world considerably . . . and I yours. Not about food. About *pits*. But we'll do that some other time.

Haven't we both ended up in places we never meant to go? Can't we find fellowship in the suffering of slipping into a gosh-awful mess? Ironically, nothing makes us feel more alone than being in a pit, yet we've got enough underground company there to displace the overpopulation of West Texas gophers and leave them homeless for years. You just can't see all those underground neighbors because of your own pit wall. In case no one near you is 'fessing up, I'LL TALK LOUD.

What I lack in knowledge I make up for in volume. Sharing some lessons learned from those pits is the least I can do after the grace I've received.

Actually, I haven't been in a pit in a long time, but right about now, I have the opportunity to go back if I want. Don't worry. I don't. It would be pretty easy to fall in if I wanted to. Don't worry. I don't want to. I'm just saying the edges are pretty slippery where I'm walking. I'm dealing with some negative experiences that could put me there in the blink of an eye. In fact, I think God has appointed me to feel the call of the pit at exactly the time I'm working on this book so I won't have to rely entirely upon memories for its content. I can tap into my own present experience and empathize with you.

I got a letter recently from a woman describing the terrible obstacles she faced. Then she proceeded to list all the wonderful things in my life and asked how someone like me had the audacity to offer advice (via Bible study) to someone like her. I didn't mind the question. She just didn't know. God has blessed me immeasurably but, to be sure, He has left some useful thorns and thistles in my yard to keep me from making myself at home in the fertilizer.

The sister who wrote me was right; she does have it tougher than I do. But I've lived long enough to know that no one has it easy. Not even that woman with the two-hundred-dollar shoes and three-hundred-dollar purse. That Prada bag on someone's shoulder may look impressive, but it still holds junk. Every person deals with secret pain. Private hurts. Some of those aches have gone on for a long time. As graciously as I knew how, I wrote the woman back and included my own list. I'll spare you the gory details as long as you promise to trust that I do have a list.

For whatever reason, most of the items on my list recently decided to stand up and be heard at once. I've learned along the way that when Satan bartends, he prefers to serve mixed drinks. You know what I mean. Cocktails of troubles. Take them one at a time and you can keep walking straight. Mixed all together, they can send you reeling.

I've given myself over to a season of deep despair only one time in my adult life. It was years ago when I first faced up to my past. Recently I've been tempted to go there again. Tempted to take a break from fighting the good fight. Tempted to sit down in my difficulties, cry "Woe is me," and wallow for a while. But I know better. I already know that if I give in to that temptation, this will be no quick-stop pity party. Satan has me registered at an extended-stay motel where I'm liable to slide from the front desk into the black hole in a split second. Nope. I'm not going into that pit. But let's just say I can see it from where I'm standing.

The whole thing started with a health issue that lasted for months and took a physical toll. The problem was finally resolved, but not without some forced alterations to my unreasonable schedule. Among other things, I had to admit my limitations and give up something I dearly love. I had to relinquish a class I had taught for twenty-two years. I'd still like to be bitter about it, but I'm too scared of God. He's trying to help me out, and if I don't let Him, I'm liable to work myself into an early grave.

Perhaps very much like you, I also have a long-term relational situation that periodically—sometimes regularly—serves up some serious pain. I always plan to handle it better, but I forget how badly the process is going to hurt. Like all of us, I want the long-term situation to be fixed once and for all, but instead it stays put like a wart on a frog.

That analogy may look like a random comparison, but frogs have been on my mind lately. We live near a pond that is home to a bellowing chorus of gargantuan green frogs. Somebody must have spiked the water with steroids, because these croakers are huge. It's not a reach to picture the frogs ending up the size of King Kong. Beanie found a dead one the other day and buried it in our backyard. Instead of decomposing like it should, the confounded thing must have petrified. Beanie keeps digging it up and burying it over and over again. It's driving me crazy.

That's how my relational challenge is. Just when I think what's causing the hurt is finally dead and buried, someone will dig it up. On a good day I know God has entrusted it to me for the purpose of refining, humbling, and breaking me where I still need to be broken. It keeps me on my toes and down on my knees all at the same time. On a bad day, as Proverbs 13:12 says, my hope seems deferred and my heart feels sick.

At first glance, we might be tempted to think a pit of despair is not a pit of sin, but the apostle Paul would beg to differ. He says that those who have the all-surpassing power of God in their meager jars of clay are "hard pressed on every side, but not crushed." We may be "perplexed but not in despair." We may be "struck down" but in the power of our indwelling Christ, we are most certainly "not destroyed" (see 2 Corinthians 4:8–9). Despair is not just sadness. It's not healthy grief. It is hopelessness. We who have Christ possess the very essence—become the very embodiment—of hope (see Romans 15:13). Hopelessness means we've believed the evil one's report over God's.

As my grandmother used to say, sometimes we need to give ourselves a good talking to. We need to speak straight to our soul where the problem resides and say something like this:

> Why are you downcast, O my soul?
> Why so disturbed within me?
> Put your hope in God,
> for I will yet praise him,
> my Savior and my God. (Psalm 42:5)

If we don't put our hope in God, we can talk ourselves into a pit. In the last twenty years of ministry, my ears have been privy to accounts of at least a thousand trips to the pit. As terrible as getting thrown into a pit can be, people never seem more frustrated and undone than when their slide into one is caused by their own ignorance or foolishness. Amid agonizing consequences, they are relentlessly haunted by what could have been avoided. Boy, do I know the feeling.

To get your wheels turning the right direction, I'll give you a handful of examples of ways you can slip into a pit. Mind you, a person doesn't have to go to some of the following extremes to end up in a pit. Remember, all a pit requires is that you feel stuck, that you feel you can't stand up effectively to your enemy, and that your vision is slowly failing. In the previous chapter we talked about the complications of getting thrown into a pit. It can be even more complicated when, instead of getting thrown in, we help ourselves into the abyss. Slip sliding away. See if any of the following examples come close to fitting you:

- You just meant to watch your weight. You certainly didn't intend to end up with an eating disorder. Nobody knows yet. Or at least that's what you think. You hope they think you're just very disciplined. You also hope that you can stop all this when you're thin enough . . . for long enough.

- You just meant to borrow the money and pay every dime of it back. You just needed to buy a little time while you were short on cash. I mean, a person has to have certain amenities. The interest was high, but you were on your way up the ladder. You never meant to end up with a mountain of debt that would throw you into bankruptcy.

- You just needed relief from your back pain so you could work. So you could enjoy your family again. You didn't intend to end up with an addiction to prescription pain killers.

- You thought you'd finally made a really good friend. Found your soul mate. The last thing you intended was to end up in a lesbian relationship. Such a thing never entered your mind.

- Your sincerest heart's desire was to minister to that person. You weren't looking for the biggest entanglement of your life. How do you get out now? You know it's not healthy, but you hate to hurt the person so badly. After all, for a while it worked for you as much as it did for her. Now you're being smothered to death.

- You were just doing business. I mean, it's a dog-eat-dog world out there, and you happen to be good at it. Sure, you knew the deal was a little "iffy" but you considered it creative financing. You certainly never meant to find yourself on a witness stand trying to keep out of prison.

◘ You just meant to have a wonderful romance. After all, you'd waited so long as you watched so many other people fall in love. It was your turn. You just wanted to be close. Plan a future with him. You didn't mean to fall into bed with him. Now you can't seem to fall out.

◘ You just meant to help your teenage son out of a few messes. You hoped each one would be the last. Every time he seemed so repentant, so sincere about not letting anything like that happen again. Everybody needs second and third chances. Everybody needs someone to believe in him. You didn't tell his dad because your son begged you not to. Anyway, you thought things would work out just fine. Now he's in a huge mess . . . and you have this sick feeling in your soul that you helped him get there.

◘ You just meant to flirt. It seemed harmless. He seemed happily married and you were too. It was all in fun, you thought. Now you're in the biggest mess of your life.

◘ You meant just to have some privacy. You'd shared enough dorm rooms and apartments. You wanted to study. Hear yourself think. Never did it dawn on you that being by yourself might leave you lonely enough to look for company on the Web. Now it's gone some place you didn't mean for it to go, and you can't seem to stop.

Of the three ways to get into a pit, I think the one I hate most is getting yourself into it. I hate the fool it makes of you. David hated it too. Empathize with his pain as he looked upon the folly that had brought him to such a low state.

> My guilt has overwhelmed me
>> like a burden too heavy to bear.
> My wounds fester and are loathsome
>> because of my sinful folly.
> I am bowed down and brought very low . . .
> All my longings lie open before you, O Lord;
>> my sighing is not hidden from you.
> My heart pounds, my strength fails me;
>> even the light has gone from my eyes . . .
> Those who seek my life set their traps . . .
> I have become like a man who does not hear,
>> whose mouth can offer no reply.
> I wait for you, O Lord;
>> you will answer, O Lord my God.
> For I said, "Do not let them gloat
>> or exalt themselves over me
>> when my foot slips."
> For I am about to fall,
>> and my pain is ever with me.
> (Psalm 38:4–6, 9–10, 12, 14–17)

Traps set. Feet slip. I hate how the enemy uses the guilt over how you got into a pit to trap you into never getting out. Hear me clearly: you cannot let him get away with that. Settle in your mind right now that staying in the pit is absolutely unacceptable. Lose it as an option. No matter how responsible and guilty you feel for sliding your way in, God wants you out. If you know Jesus Christ personally, you are not stuck. You do have the power to stand up against the enemy.

God still has a vision for you. No matter where you've been, God's full intent is for you to live effectively (see John 15:8) and abundantly (see John 10:10). He loves you dearly, and the fact that you've been foolish doesn't diminish His love one single ounce. This time, instead of giving yourself a good talking-to, use your mouth to talk to God. Echo the words of the psalmist when he cried:

> If I should say, "My foot has slipped,"
>> Your lovingkindness, O Lord, will
> hold me up.
>> When my anxious thoughts multiply
> within me,
>> Your consolations delight my soul.
> (Psalm 94:18–19 nasb)

If you don't soak your brain in the truth that you are absolutely secure in the unchanging love of God, you will never feel worthy of getting out of the pit. Satan will keep your feet on slippery ground. When you want out of your pit, you've got a golden opportunity to see the grace of God as you've never encountered it. Let God's loving-kindness hold you up and ask Him to make His consolations your delight.

In some of the chapters that follow we'll get more specific about how to get out of a pit, but for now I want you to concentrate on a gift you can bring out with you. Think of it as the door prize. Your diamond in the rough. Your plunder from the pit. In every one of the scenarios I listed above, Satan used ignorance to get the person near enough to the mouth of the pit for him or her to slip in. One of the most priceless gifts we can bring out of our pit is newfound knowledge. Simply put, we can be a whole lot smarter coming out than we were going in. We are no longer innocent, but we have the opportunity before us to trade in our innocence for integrity. If we're willing, we can come out of the pit smartened up to Satan's agenda.

We can also tell on him to anyone who will listen. That's what I'm trying to do. When Scripture speaks of the devil's schemes, it speaks of a well-contrived program based on a step-by-step progressive plan (see Ephesians 6:10–12). Though he tailors the specifics to fit individual weaknesses, I believe Satan's basic progressive plan remains consistent.

Distraction ➲ Addiction ➲ Destruction

Satan's definitive goal is to reap destruction, but that's rarely his starting point. His usual opening is distraction. Scripture has a name for a small distraction that becomes a big distraction. It's called a *stronghold*. Scripture defines it as any and "every pretension that sets itself up against the knowledge of God" (2 Corinthians 10:5). Anything that becomes a bigger preoccupation in your mind than the truth and knowledge of God, anything that dwarfs His truth and knowledge in your imagination, is a stronghold. In other words, if I have a relationship through which I can no longer prioritize Christ and His Word, Satan is building a stronghold there. If watching what I eat is no longer a means to better health and instead has become a major preoccupation, Satan is building a stronghold. If a same-sex friendship takes on a dimension of jealousy usually limited to a male-female romance, Satan is building a stronghold.

Get the picture? He has no intention of allowing the new focus to remain a simple distraction. The next step is addiction. You see, a stronghold is something we *have*. A pit is somewhere we *live* . . . if only for a while. An addiction is a highly effective way for something you have (a sin-induced problem) to turn into some place you live (a sin-induced pit). Defeat becomes a lifestyle. In Ephesians 4:18–19, the apostle Paul issued a strong warning to believers to no longer be like those who are "darkened in their understanding and separated from the life of God because of the ignorance that is in them due to the hardening of their hearts. Having lost all sensitivity, they have given themselves over to sensuality so as to indulge in every kind of impurity, with a continual lust for more."

What is true in the realm of sensuality is equally true in all other areas of repetitive sin. The present level of satisfaction will soon lose its sensitivity. We will need to indulge in more. Then a little more. In doing so, we become caught in the furious cycle of continual lust. That, my friend, is an addiction. Glance at the Scripture again, because you don't want to miss the fact that it all started with ignorance. Even the people described in the verse, as rebellious as they may have been, drove into a pit beyond their original intention.

A person can be addicted to substances, behaviors, *and* relationships. (Many of us have learned all too painfully that emotional addictions can be as overwhelming as physical addictions.) Satan is smug about his progress at this point but remember, addiction is not his goal. Destruction is. He wants to destroy our lives, our callings, our sense of godly significance, our personal intimacy with God, and every relationship that matters to us. He doesn't do it all at once where the evil of his plan is obvious. The movement toward destruction is progressive, from one tiny step to the next in little increments that you don't even notice.

Satan is a master at what he does, but he is not without limits. Listen carefully: if you belong to Christ, Satan cannot destroy *you*. The best he can do is to convince you that you're destroyed. No, beloved, you're not. No matter what's happened. No matter how foolish you've been. No matter how far you've gone. Wise up. The enemy is lying to you. Yes, he may have inflicted some tremendous losses. He did that to me. He may even have destroyed your job and torn apart some precious relationships—at least for now. But out of the unfathomable mercies of God, what you stand to gain if you're willing to lift up your empty hands to Him is astonishing.

To wise up to Satan's progressive plan, we want to discern the early warning signals of a dangerous distraction and be onto him. Look back at the list of pit-slipping scenarios above, and you'll notice that many of them began innocently. Take the first five, for instance. It's not a sin to watch your weight. It's not a sin to get a loan. It's not a sin to seek relief from chronic physical pain that is robbing you of all quality of life. For crying out loud, it's certainly not a sin to make good friendships. And what does Christ want more than for us to minister to others? Somewhere along the way in each of these cases, Satan capitalized on an area of ignorance and detoured a healthy drive into a deep ditch.

My daughter, Amanda, made a good friend in college that I have come to love as much as she does. Michelle is not only an avid lover of God, she can play a good, clean practical joke like no one I know. When she was at Texas A&M six years ago, she lived with some girlfriends in an apartment just a few doors down from four other buddies. She found the gullibility of these neighboring girls so delightfully inviting that she and her apartment mates contrived a plan. It began with swiping small things from their apartment. Knickknacks, small vases, and the like. Just as she hoped, they didn't notice. Soon she moved on to bigger and better things: small pictures, flower arrangements, etc. Again, not a word. Ah, the fun had begun. She progressed to obvious things like taking a framed picture off the wall. She grinned ear to ear with accomplishment when she recalled the coup de grâce: dragging one of their breakfast room chairs right out from under their noses. The unsuspecting victims never said a word.

Beside themselves with victory, Michelle and her roommates soon issued an invitation to their neighbors to join them for dinner. The décor was arranged to make them feel right at home. Every knickknack was displayed. Every framed picture in open view. The flower arrangement on the table. And at the very head of the table? Ah, yes: the victory chair.

Oh, the joy of victor's spoils! We laughed our heads off as Michelle described the looks on their friends' faces as the light dawned. Their eyes jumped from one thing to another like the steel ball in a pinball machine. They looked at each other and then at their hosts, chirping madly, "Hey, that's mine!"

You gotta love it. Till somebody who hates you does it. Somebody powerful. Somebody sinister. Somebody who does it for a living . . . and does it well. You and I have got to be onto the enemy's schemes when he swipes the first knickknack. We need desperately to discern when our souls take the first hit and make an immediate adjustment. For example, when you realize a relationship you've just begun is going to be dangerous and destructive, you can bow out before you get any closer. Or if you realize your job places you in a virtually undetectable position to use money, and you're in a financially vulnerable situation right now, set up safeguards and automatic accountability. Live out in the light. Don't just practice innocence. Practice integrity.

The last thing God wants is for you and me to live in fear. Undoubtedly "the one who is in you [the Holy Spirit] is greater than the one who is in the world [Satan]" (1 John 4:4). We don't want to be afraid, but we've got to be alert. If you're in Christ, you have a built-in alarm system. The Holy Spirit is in us, and if we don't quench Him He'll tell us early on when we're headed for trouble. He'll also tell us whether to be careful right where we are or to bail out altogether.

A few weeks ago my buddy Vicky was getting ready for work when she heard a beeper going off somewhere in her house. She was a tad perplexed, since she doesn't own a beeper. She reasoned it was her husband's, knew he'd be in trouble without it, and started trying to find it. The sound was so loud that she was sure it must be in the room with her, but she searched in vain. She looked under the cushions of her couch and chairs. She looked behind the TV. She exhausted one room and looked in another. No matter where Vicky went, the sound was the same. No "getting hotter," no "getting colder." Just a steady beep. Imagine her surprise when she finally realized that the beep was coming from inside of her. The battery on her pacemaker was going out and sounding an alarm. She didn't even know the pacemaker had an alarm.

You may not know you have one either, but you do. When it goes off, you've got to learn to listen to it. The hardest part may be that you won't always understand why the beeper is going off—why God is directing you to back off from a situation or a relationship. The warning may not make any human sense. When this happens, beware of rationalizing yourself into a pit! Mind what the Holy Spirit is telling you even if you don't know why. You may live on for years without clear understanding, but you can praise God by faith, knowing He veered your car a different direction to keep you out of some kind of ditch.

Another way you can sometimes recognize Satan at work is that you begin to feel backed into a corner. Unfortunately, this is not an early sign, but it can often be a sure sign. It's ironic Satan tries to sell us the philosophy that God wants to squelch us and confine us and that, like Him, we should be able to do whatever we want. The serpent slithered that philosophy into the soil of the Garden. Satan promises wide-open spaces, but then he backs us into a pit.

If a new relationship or opportunity is causing you to feel trapped or backed into a corner, God could be flagging you that Satan is all over it. God issues dos and don'ts, but always for freedom's sake. Psalm 18:36 says of our God, "You enlarge my steps under me, / And my feet have not slipped" (NASB). Satan backs us into a corner on slippery ground strategically close to the nearest pit. God enlarges our steps under us, enabling us to see a pit from a greater distance so we don't have to live in constant dread of falling into another one.

Nothing gives me greater joy than for one of my children to share something God has been saying to them. One of my favorite examples of this dovetailed from a near disaster. When Melissa was a senior in high school, Satan plotted her path right into a pit and steered her toward it. She was a slim and darling size 6 before a series of unhappy incidents caused her some deep sadness. She lost her appetite and dropped down to a size 2. At one point she could even wear a size 0. Mind you, she was 5′8″ tall. (Incidentally, the thinner she got, the more affirmation she got from her peers.)

The nightmare didn't start with an eating issue but it certainly ended up there. Keith and I were scared half to death. Needless to say, we sought God with everything we had. We received godly counsel, prayed Scriptures over her, and fought the enemy ferociously. I am so thankful Satan didn't get Melissa anywhere near the finish line he planned for her. After a few excruciating months, she came to a place where she wanted out of that pit. She called upon her God relentlessly, and He came to her rescue. Melissa emerged from that pit with a gift.

She couldn't get enough of God's Word. Her ticket out turned into her soul's delight. Scriptures that seem as old and familiar as a worn out bathrobe to some people came totally alive to Melissa.

One day she called me on the cell phone and blurted, "Are you ready for this?" In those days that tone was limited entirely to a fresh revelation that had come to her. I grinned, sat back, and replied, "Hit me."

"Mother, did you know that God prepares a table before me in the presence of my enemy?" Her newfound passion had obviously led her to stumble onto the Twenty-Third Psalm. "And get this" she bubbled. "He forces my enemy to watch as He anoints my head with oil!" The enemy had gotten one over on Melissa. She was ecstatic to be getting one over on him.

Beloved, listen up a minute. God prepares a table before you in the presence of your enemy too. And guess what? It can be decorated and surrounded by every single knickknack, vase, flower arrangement, and picture Satan stole from your place. You can sit right down in that chair—the one he dragged out of your house right under your nose. And don't you get up from that chair until God anoints you with an overflow of the Holy Spirit that only comes to those most desperate for Him. Right in front of your enemy's eyes.

Look at it this way: the fact that you are reading this book—or anything like it—betrays that Satan didn't take you anywhere near the finish line he planned for you. When you slipped into that pit, you went to a place you never intended. Now you're going to a place *Satan* never intended. Don't you stop until the enemy is sorry he ever messed with you.

out of

the MUD and MIRE;

CHAPTER FOUR

When You Jump Into a Pit

You can jump in. That's the third and final way you can land in a pit. Before you take the plunge into that pit, you can be well aware that what you're about to do is wrong, probably even foolish. But for whatever reason, the escalating desire to do it exceeds the good sense not to. Unlike the second route into a pit, you didn't just slip in before you knew what was happening. You had time to think, and then you did exactly what you meant to do even if the pit turned out to be deeper and the consequences higher than you hoped.

Don't start squirming and think I'm about to talk down to you. Believe me, I've jumped into my share of pits. Based on the results of the three test groups I mentioned in chapter one, I can assure you that so have most other people. If I asked you the same questions, you, too, could likely raise a hand of affirmation to all three pit-landing scenarios. Yep, at some point in our lives we've been thrown into a pit. At another, we slipped into a pit. And at still another we hauled off, aimed, and jumped square into the bull's-eye of a pit.

Throughout this entire chapter I want you to keep in mind that I lived a vast measure of my life cycling from one pit to another. I've made the trip all three ways and numerous times. Wherever you've been, I've probably been there too. Our paths to that pit and our length of stay may have differed, but I can't imagine that you sank any deeper than I did.

I'd be a hypocrite to talk down to you, but I'd like to ask your permission to talk straight to you. If I don't tell it like it really is, you'll just tune out what I have to say like you've tuned out countless others who said the same thing, but so properly you ignored them. I know how that is.

A wall as thin as a potato chip separates my desk from the orthodontist's office next door. He's the one who keeps me in a retainer to restrain the overwhelming propensity of my two front teeth to overbite. I once had the worst buckteeth in the free world, so I appreciate a good orthodontist as much as anyone. And I appreciate his staff. In fact, I practically know their entire life histories, because the sound carries so clearly through those walls they may as well be talking in my office. Should any of them get into legal trouble, I could serve as a character witness.

I can vouch for their integrity, but they're a bit remiss on updating their patients' instructional videos. The same instructions for wearing and caring for your braces have sifted through that wall so many times I could recite them line for line. Day in, day out the video drones until my head starts nodding forward and I suddenly wake myself up snoring. I know the challenge of flossing correctly when you have braces. I know the tendency of an unseemly food pileup on the top teeth. I know exactly where to put the rubber bands and what happens if you don't. I know the benefits of headgear and how they can cut your brace time in half. And I no longer care. In fact, I'm so bored I'd cast my retainer to the wind except for fear my teeth would revert so badly I'd spill my Starbucks every time I took a sip.

I know what happens when you hear the same old thing the same old way. So you're not going to get a tired old overbite rerun from me. I'm going to try a different approach. If I didn't care, I would save myself the trouble. After all, by nature I'm a people pleaser. The thing is I now know what I needed at my own times of pit-jumping, and few people in my life had the guts to give it. I also happen to know that if jumping in a pit is your *modus operandi*, you're probably cynical enough not to respect me if I don't spit it out.

In fact (and, mind you, I'm still talking straight, not down), if you are a confirmed pit-jumper, you've probably got a pretty serious authority problem over all. Forgive my amateur psychology, but my guess is that your primary authority figure was or is either a wimp or a fraud. God is neither. He knows what it will take to get your attention, and He's willing to do it. Trust me. I know this from personal experience. I also know the games we play with one another as we make excuses for our gross inconsistencies. Especially we churchy types. So, if you don't mind, I'll spare us both the useless decorum and get right to the point.

When all is said and done, you, like me, probably do what you do because you want to. You ordinarily jump in a pit because you like the trip. No, you don't necessarily like the cost but, like all vacations, a great trip can be worth the expense. It looks good. It feels good. Or it tastes good. It just doesn't last nearly long enough, which is why we come back and take the next trip.

Stay with me here, beloved. Surely you know that it takes one to know one. The only reason I'm not still in a pit is because, after many warnings, God mushroomed such devastating consequences of sin and emotional unhealthiness that it nearly killed me—did kill the old me, as a matter of fact. As Job 33:29–30 says:

> God does all these things to a man—
> twice, even three times—
> to turn back his soul from the pit,
> that the light of life may shine on him.

God brought me to a place where I was willing to do anything to get out of the pit and everything to stay out. To be out of the mud and mire and have my feet upon a rock became what I wanted more than anything in the world. If you have the same tendency toward pit-jumping, I wish more than anything to talk you into crying out for deliverance before you reach the point I did. Before your world as you know it comes tumbling down. Praise God, He is the rebuilder of ruins, but surely there are easier ways to get a new home than to let an emotional tornado tear the old one to pieces.

Remember that road trip I told you about in Chapter one? Keith's well-worn atlas led us for a time through the northwest corner of the great state of Nebraska. It was early afternoon, and we knew the weather looked a little foreboding. But we're from the coast where storms come and go so regularly that, unless it's a bad one, we hardly notice. We hadn't stopped in several hours and finally saw a road sign marking an upcoming rest stop. Both Keith and I needed to rest especially badly.

When we stopped I started fishing around the SUV for leashes, because Sunny and Beanie no doubt needed to rest as well. The wind was blowing so hard that when I opened the car door, it swung forward with a force I feared would bend the hinges. The doggy rest area was an unfortunate distance away and Beanie, as fraidy cat of a dog as you'll ever meet, got so scared she couldn't rest. Sunny, on the other hand, braved a gale-force wind that bugged her eyes and slicked her fur until she looked like a sumo wrestler with a too-tight ponytail. I got so tickled I had to shove the dogs back in the truck and hurry to rest.

"Good grief! Is it windy enough in Nebraska?" I asked as I hopped back in the car and threw on my seat belt.

We'd driven only a minute or so when Keith, with eyes as wide as a wildcat, said, "Lizabeth, look behind us!" I turned and saw a huge, loose funnel cloud spinning between the rest stop and us. We were floored. So was the gas pedal. We did get our usual coffee later that afternoon, but we didn't really need it. Believe me, we were no longer traveling on mental autopilot. We were wide awake.

What if you woke up today from the autopilot of poor decisions? What if a domestic tornado didn't have to huff and puff and blow your house down to get your attention? What if, before the bottom fell out, you would respond to a Voice in the wilderness saying, "Stop it!" (see Isaiah 1:16)? And what if that same Voice—the only One that matters—was willing to tell you how to stop?

That could happen. In fact, if we were willing to let it, it would happen. God in His tender mercy gives us plenty of warnings enabling us to avoid pits, but the problem with us pit-jumpers is that we don't want to hear those warnings. We want what we want. So we stick our fingers in our ears before we jump in.

What on earth drives us to do such a thing? Of all the ways into the pit, jumping in is by far the most dangerous and the most supremely—oh, that I had an even stronger word!—*consequential.* You see, motive is huge to God. So is character.

Primarily His character, which we are created to emulate. And He will not be mocked. The very segment of Scripture where we're told God won't be mocked is strategically centered in the context of reaping what we sow (see Galatians 6:7–9). We can't fool Him by hiding our inner motive. God looks intently not only at what we've done and how, but also at *why* we did it. The Bible tells us that, unlike people, God doesn't look on the outward appearance of things. He looks upon the heart. First Chronicles 28:9 says, "the LORD searches every heart and understands every motive behind the thoughts."

Do you want to hear something ironic? This very aspect of God (His omniscience) that helps save our scrawny necks when we've slipped into a pit (we didn't mean to) nearly hangs us when we've jumped into it (we did mean to, no matter what story we're telling). If you've ever made that jump, I really don't have to tell you that you had your reasons. You did it because of something you wanted. I'll just throw out a token few common reasons here for good measure. Maybe you can find your own somewhere on the list. A pit-jumper . . .

- Wanted to steal the money
- Meant to cheat the company
- Wanted to go to bed with that person
- Wanted to have the affair
- Wanted to take vengeance
- Set out to hurt that person

- Went into that relationship knowing full well that person was an unbeliever . . . or had a dark side
- Wanted to experience something illicit
- Wanted to get drunker than a skunk. Higher than a kite. Lower than a snake's belly

You get the picture. Psalm 19:13 gives a couple of names to pit-jumping. Facing his own bent for jumping into pits (oh, that we'd all do that!), the psalmist pled with God:

> Keep Your servant from willful sins;
> do not let them rule over me.
> Then I will be innocent,
> and cleansed from blatant rebellion. (HCSB)

Willful sins. Blatant rebellion. The two are as tied together as a bird and a feather. Innate in every act of rebellion is an authority figure we're rebelling against. Hence, my hunch that if you—like the old me—keep choosing the left turn over and over again, you've got an authority problem. I know I did. We're desperate to ask God to help us overcome it. Even after we do, you and I are never going to be able to submit to authority perfectly as long as our feet of clay are stuck to Planet Earth.

But don't let anybody—particularly someone touting a twisted doctrine of grace—talk you into thinking you can't be liberated from willful sin and blatant rebellion just because he or she hasn't been. I know for a fact that you can be completely set free from every sin that rules over you. Then and only then will you and I possess the kind of innocence possible for Homo sapiens still inhaling terrestrial air.

To get there, we not only need some deep repentance (in essence, a change of mind resulting in a change of direction), we need some marrow-deep healing, or we'll simply change right back. Contrary to popular opinion, yes, even people who plan sin and strategically jump into pits need healing. In fact, maybe we need it most of all. No one needs the Physician more than the person who likes the taste of the toxin that keeps poisoning her.

I stumbled onto a name for our problem just recently while perusing a commentary on James 1:13–15. Before we delve into that name, a fresh reading of the Scripture wouldn't hurt us, so I'll start there:

> When tempted, no one should say, "God is tempting me." For God cannot be tempted by evil, nor does he tempt anyone; but each one is tempted when, by his own evil desire, he is dragged away and enticed. Then, after desire has conceived, it gives birth to sin, and sin, when it is full-grown, gives birth to death.

The original Greek word translated "evil desire" is *epithumia*. Actually, the word is neutral and can be used for right desires as well as wrong ones. Christ used the word in Luke 22:15 when He "eagerly desired to eat" the Passover with His disciples. By itself the term *epithumia* simply means a strong or passionate desire. The context, as in James 1:14, determines whether or not the desire is wrong. Here's the interesting part: the *New American Commentary* defines *epithumia* in this Scripture segment as "deformed desire."[1]

Let that phrase settle on you for a minute.

You see, that's what I had. Deformed desire. In my own pit-jumping (as opposed to pit-slipping), I often ended up doing exactly what I set out to do . . . what at that moment or in that season I thought I *wanted* to do. Like you, perhaps, I wished I didn't want the things I did. I often hated what I wanted. Still, desire—deformed and destructive—lurched and led. Isaiah 44:20 describes the kind of person I was:

> He feeds on ashes, a deluded heart misleads him;
>> he cannot save himself, or say,
>> "Is not this thing in my right hand a lie?"

I had thought of my heart as only sinful. I didn't realize that deeper still, underneath that film of soil, my heart was sick. One of the most important shifts in my belief system began with the realization that I had a messed up "want to." My desires were tremendously unhealthy. Self-destructive. In the language of the *New American Commentary*, I had "deformed desires."

I'm not the only one. I have a good friend who graciously invited me into her harrowingly self-destructive mind. Self-destruction was my thing, too, but her emotional elevator plunged her to an even lower floor. After spending ninety days in jail for a second DUI, she expressed to me that the whole time she was there, she never had any other plan than to walk out that door and get a drink. She reasoned that the only thing she needed to do differently was perhaps not drive.

After getting out she got too drunk to keep her appointments with her probation officer and ended up spending a third gig behind bars, this time for six months. A few days after release? Same thing.

In light of all she'd lost—job, marriage, kids, self-respect—her walking out the door and doing the same thing again baffled me. I asked her why she had done it. Hadn't the relentless demand of her internal organs finally had time to die down? She said dryly, "Because I wanted to. Beth, I don't think you're listening. I wanted to drink. I liked how it made me feel."

Or how it made her *not* feel.

Deformed desires. The desire to *not* desire is one of the most deformed desires we'll ever have. One of the biggest mistakes we could ever make is to assume that passionate desire is wrong, and that the goal for godly people is to not feel. Nothing could be further from the truth. We were created out of holy passion *for* holy passion. So perfectly fitted for passion are we that we will find it one way or another. If we don't find it in Christ, we'll find it in things like lust, anger, rage, and greed.

Never minimize the power of desire. Though doing what you need to do is the place to start, you'll never make it in the long haul motivated by need alone. The most self-disciplined among us may walk in victory for a few weeks out of our need to do the right thing, but it will rarely carry us to the finish line. Each of us will ultimately do what we want to do.

Is it any wonder that the first words of Christ recorded in the incomparable Gospel of John are, "What do you want?" Hear Him echo the same words to you today. "What do *you* want, child?" What are your secret desires? Place them before Him. Name every single one. No matter how healthy or unhealthy. No matter how respectable. No matter how deformed. I am proof that God can heal the most messed up "want to." In recent years no verse has meant more to me than Psalm 40:8: "I delight to do Your will, O my God; / Your Law is within my heart" (NASB).

I still can hardly fathom that I can say those words and mean them after where I've been. God healed my deformed desires, finally getting through my thick skull that the things He wanted for me were the best things life could offer. Using the hammer of His Word and the anvil of His unfailing love, God reshaped my disfigured desires until what I wanted more than anything on earth was what He wanted. Somewhere along the way, God's "law" transferred from the stone tablets of my head to the soft tissue of my heart. I bought in—not just spiritually, but emotionally. Jesus finally, completely, won my heart. And not just mine. Remember that good friend I told you about who wanted that next drink regardless of the consequences? I've never known anyone in more bondage. Christ finally got through to her, won her heart, and changed her desires. She's a miracle. I'm a miracle. If He can deliver the two of us, He can deliver anyone.

So much of our propensity toward pit-jumping springs from the fact that somewhere down deep inside, we just don't trust God. We think He's like all the others who have cheated or betrayed us. As my friend, Chris Thom, says, "God is not just a big us." Like Adam and Eve, we let the enemy taunt us into believing God is holding out on us. Our drive for the proverbial forbidden fruit is our innate belief that what we are denied is exactly what we want most.

Satan was a liar then, and he's a liar now.

In my research for this book, I learned that certain kinds of relationships and people become automatic pits for us the second we intimately engage. For instance, Proverbs 22:14 warns, "The mouth of forbidden women is a deep pit" (ESV). The same is true of forbidden men. A relationship that is so enticing to us precisely because it's forbidden is nothing but a decoratively painted door to a cavernous pit. Scripture could not paint a more vivid picture: their very mouths are deep pits. Place your mouth on one of those and you kiss your solid ground good-bye. God doesn't just say no because it makes Him feel good about Himself. God feels fine about Himself. He doesn't need us to feel small so He can feel big. He's huge. He doesn't have to be bossy to feel like the boss. He's the master of the universe. If God forbids something, the sooner we believe and confess that it's for our sakes, the better off we'll be.

Proverbs 23:27 adds that "a prostitute is a deep pit; / an adulteress is a narrow well" (ESV). The King James Version uses a far stronger word than "prostitute"—stronger even than the American Standard Version's "harlot"—and one that suggests that the term isn't limited to someone who is paid to have sex. It refers to anyone who sleeps around and practices immorality as a virtual lifestyle. Needless to say, the verse is equally true in gender reversal. A man who sleeps around is a deep pit, and an adulterer is a narrow well. Mess with them and, in a manner of speaking, you'll hurl yourself in the bowels of the earth with such meteoric force that only God can pull you out. I don't care how flattering someone's attention may be. If he or she is immoral or married to somebody else, an intimate relationship of any kind with that person will automatically—not probably or eventually—hurl you into a pit. ETA? Instantly.

Based on everything the Word of God says and every-thing I've experienced, heard, or observed, I promise you that forbidden relationships never turn out well. Let me say that one more time: *never*. The pit is deep and dark. And before you know it, you'll find that you are in it all alone. I've also lived long enough and listened hard enough to become convinced that we are almost always right, no matter how we don't want to be, when we get a nagging feeling somewhere down inside that a person to whom we're growing increasingly attached has a serious dark side. That's the Holy Spirit warning us. Learn to associate darkness with a pit. I say all of this to you out of deep love and concern. Repent and run.

Keep in mind that automatic pit-jumping can be circum-stantial and relational, and it also has a far broader range than matters of sexuality. Forbidden sexual relationships simply trigger some of the boldest scriptural guarantees of disaster. The wider context is anything that God goes to the trouble to forbid.

He's actually a "yes" kind of God (see 2 Corinthians 1:20). You can mark this one down any time and every time: God's "no" is a quick shove away from a pit. The sooner the shove, the better.

I didn't begin to live in victory just because all opportunity to jump finally disappeared. That's not the case at all. While I was still at greatest risk, God stayed on me, worked with me, and built trust in me until finally I'd go where He pointed.

That's been our MO for a while, but He's wise to never let me forget the excruciating pain of where I've been ... lest I be tempted to go back. Until we're nine-tenths in the grave, none of us is past the danger of a pit.

Get a load of the words out of King David's mouth immediately after promising God he'd lead a blameless life: "When will you come to me?" (Psalm 101:2). Translation? "I don't know how long I can keep this up. Are you coming soon? Killing me soon? Can't we pit-jumpers relate? Quick carnal impulses leap into all of our heads at times, but once we've let God win our hearts, a high tide of holy desire can come and wash them away like jellyfish swept from the shore.

Recently at a speaking engagement, a group of women gave me a Barbie. It wasn't the first. I think the joke started after I told the story of my young friend, Savannah, who often sits with me at church. She's a grown-up eleven now, but when she was about six and seven she loved to bring her Barbies to church. I'm happy to say that she dressed them in their more modest outfits. Of course, there was that one time when a skirt was so short I had to wrap an offering envelope around her hips. I had to remind myself that sanctification is a process, and some Barbies need extra time for change to become observable. I was one of them.

As long as Savannah's Barbies were at church, I surmised they might as well engage in worship, so she and I postured them accordingly. We either held them in front of us where they could face the worship team or propped them against the back of the pew. Either way, we always lifted up their hands. Since their mouths wouldn't open and their knees wouldn't bend, we felt hand lifting to be our only recourse. Barbie elbows don't bend either, so their praise was highly demonstrative for our conservative congregation.

As far as I know, no one registered a complaint. Had they done so, I would undoubtedly have heard—like I did the time somebody turned me in for having vanilla flavoring at my Bible study's coffee bar. Took a picture of it, in fact, and slapped it on my pastor's desk. Claimed it looked like we were spiking our coffee. Help me, Jesus! You'll be glad to know that my pastor laughed.

Vanilla lattes aside, somehow the large group with whom I shared the Barbie account found it amusing and the theme caught on. I've been receiving Barbies ever since.

This most recent Barbie was dressed like me (hip, I hope, but alas, modest). She had a makeshift Bible in one hand (appeared to be a King James) while the other was stretched decisively heavenward. This doll had one inadvertent similarity to me that overrode all the others. It even made up for the gross age discrepancy no one seemed willing to acknowledge. One of Barbie's feet had been gnawed right off at the calf. The group extended their regrets, of course, explaining that the family dog of the original owner had gotten hold of the doll the day before they left. They were understandably disappointed but decided the doll was, by and large, no worse for the wear.

I stared at the Barbie for a minute. She looked so strange at first. So well coiffed, so fitted for her calling, and yet she had a gnawed-off foot. Then I nodded. Not to anyone else really. Just to God. Well, maybe also to Barbie. Though the group didn't know it, they'd hit the nail right on the head, or maybe the leg right on the stump. That was me all right.

No, I don't have a missing leg, but if you could see me with your spiritual eyes, surely at least one of my legs is gnawed off at the knee. Ephesians 4:27 warns, "Do not give the devil a foothold." Uh, too late. Satan has wounded me, but he hasn't devoured me. He got the leg, but he's never gotten the thigh, though goodness knows he wanted it. I may walk with a spiritual limp, but thanks be to God, who holds me up and urges me to lean on Him, at least I can walk. So can you. Walk away from that pit before it's the death of you.

With love, Beth.

HE set my FEET on a ROCK

CHAPTER FIVE

Getting Out of Your Pit

You can get out. Regardless of whether you were thrown in, you slipped in, or you jumped in, you can get out. And I do mean *you*. I'm not talking about the person who seems to deal with her pit better than you do. We don't need to deal with our pits. We need to get out of our pits. You can do it. Even if you have a history of failed attempts. Even if you don't think you deserve it. Even if you've never lived anywhere else.

But here's the catch: you can't get yourself out. Try as you may, you will never successfully pull yourself out of a pit. Not the kind the Word of God is talking about. Remember the number one characteristic of a pit? Mud and mire. The quicksand kind that gulp your feet whole. You're stuck. As much as you'd like to, as self-sufficient as you'd like to be, as smug as it would make you, you can't do this one alone. Somebody else has to come to your rescue. But there you have options. You can opt for human help or you can opt for God.

The fact that we could actually see our deliverer could be a decisive advantage. Just to have an audible conversation would be great. To know someone really was listening would help. To see the look on a face or hear the tone in a voice. Now, to us, that's real help.

But help alone is not what we're talking about. God meant for people to offer one another a helping hand. The trouble comes when we insist upon someone equally human becoming our deliverer. Another person—rare though he may be—really can pull us out of a pit but, for the life of him, he can't set us free.

Take Joseph, for instance. Maybe you remember that the first time Scripture mentions a pit, Joseph was in it. While he was kicking and screaming in the waterless bottom, his brothers looked up from their picnic lunch and

> saw a caravan of Ishmaelites coming from Gilead. Their camels were loaded with spices, balm and myrrh, and they were on their way to take them down to Egypt. Judah said to his brothers, "What will we gain if we kill our brother and cover up his blood? Come, let's sell him to the Ishmaelites and not lay our hands on him; after all, he is our brother, our own flesh and blood." His brothers agreed. So when the Midianite merchants came by, his brothers pulled Joseph up out of the cistern and sold him for twenty shekels of silver to the Ishmaelites, who took him to Egypt. (Genesis 37:25–28)

Agreed, getting sold into slavery was a far better option than starving to death in the bottom of the cistern. But a kind soul will give the brothers too much credit for their compassion without Psalm 105:18 to round out the picture. We're told that the Ishmaelites "bruised his feet with shackles, / his neck was put in irons." Don't forget, Joseph was only seventeen. Pampered and spoiled at that. He'd probably never even made up his pallet in the morning. Suddenly, at the drop of a head wrap, he was a slave in shackles heading who knows where.

Scripture leaves no doubt that the sovereignty of God was in full pendulum swing, directing every detail from Canaan to Egypt for the common good. Years passed, however, before Joseph began to grasp the work of his true Deliverer. In our relational parallel, if a man—or woman—pulls us out of the pit, solely assuming the role of deliverer, he or she will inadvertently sell us into slavery of one kind or another almost every time. Scripture records several instances when God heard the cries of His people and raised up a human deliverer for them instead of insisting, as He did at other times, that they look to Him alone. Each time Israel invariably returned to captivity. Psalm 78 records a disturbing record of Israel's cycle of defeat—as great a human tragedy as you'll ever read: "In spite of all [God's] wonders, they did not believe. / So he ended their days in futility" (vv. 32, 33). Here's the important part: "They did not believe in God or trust *his deliverance*" (v. 22, emphasis mine). Though God raised up leaders like Moses and Joshua, the nation still eventually defaulted to its old pattern.

I know the feeling. I had a few great leaders along the way, too, but they couldn't rewire my hard drive. I'd eventually default every time. Nothing is more futile or leaves us more fractured than trusting man to be our god. Sometimes we forget what a mistake this was the last time we did it. Time has a way of distorting our memories. That's what happened to Israel. Not many years after the writer of Psalm 78 put pen to parchment, Israel found herself scrambling for help as she faced imminent takeover by the massive army of the Assyrians. God could have thwarted the assault in a blink of His holy eye, but stayed His hand, awaiting their cry of repentance. He'd said:

> In repentance and rest is your salvation,
> in quietness and trust is your strength,
> but you would have none of it. (Isaiah 30:15)

Been there too. Rather than humble themselves and do what was required for true protection and restoration, Israel preferred calling upon the Egyptians for protection. While history etched a stark warning, they slapped a coat of gloss over their past and decided Egypt wasn't all that bad. Particularly when compared to the threatening Assyrians. They figured they'd ally with Egypt and she would deliver them. Isaiah 30 records God's response:

> "Woe to the obstinate children,"
>> declares the LORD,
>> "to those who carry out plans that are not mine,
>>> forming an alliance, but not by my Spirit,
>>> heaping sin upon sin;
>> who go down to Egypt
>>> without consulting me;
>>> who look for help to Pharaoh's protection,
>>> to Egypt's shade for refuge.
>> But Pharaoh's protection will be to your shame,
>>> Egypt's shade will bring you disgrace . . .
>> everyone will be put to shame
>>> because of a people useless to them."
> (vv. 1-3, 5)

Israel didn't need Egypt. She needed God. At his best, man can make a mighty fine man, but he's a useless god. Contrary to the serpent's suggestion in the Garden, people simply can't be divine. The higher the expectation we have for them, the further they're going to fall. (And somehow, when it's all over we feel disgraced. Embarrassed. Sometimes we don't even know why.)

People can help us but they can't heal us. People can lift us but they can't carry us. On occasion people can pull us out of a pit, but they cannot keep us out. Nor can they set our feet upon a rock. When we come out of a pit, if our idea of stability is standing on another human's shoulders, his clay feet will inevitably crumble and we'll take a tumble. The job's too big for him.

Since pit-dwelling is primarily a state of mind, effective deliverance also takes the ability to read people's minds, because what we say often doesn't match where we are. Only God can hang with us through the length and depth of our need. And the length and depth of our baloney. Maybe I'm just talking about myself, but whether or not I realized it, I usually found a way to frame my pit to make me look like a victim. Not only is God omniscient, His Word is "sharper than any double-edged sword" cutting our baloney so thin He can see straight through it. He knows when we're kidding others. He knows when we're kidding ourselves. Knowing all we are, all we feel, and all we hide, God overflows with love and willingness to deliver us. Even after Israel sought the help of the Egyptians, inviting the chastisement of God, Isaiah 30 testified, "Yet the LORD longs to be gracious to you; / he rises to show you compassion" (v. 18).

Longs to be gracious. I like the ring of that. We're also repeatedly told that "His love endures forever" which means the Lord is gracious for *long*. That's what former pit-dwellers like me must have. We need a Deliverer who is in for the long haul. Philippians 1:6 tells us that God, who began a good work, is faithful to complete it. Frankly, work doesn't get harder than pit-dweller pulling. Man, who may begin a good work, wears out too fast to finish it. And rightly he should. It's not his job. True delivery takes some time, some titanic effort, and more patience than the best of people possess. You and I need a strong arm and a long arm.

The apostle Paul described God's tenacity in 2 Corinthians 1:10 when he said, "He *has* delivered us . . . he *will* deliver us. On him we have set our hope that he will *continue* to deliver us" (emphasis mine). Past. Present. Future. That's the kind of deliverance from the pit you and I are looking for. We've got to have a lifetime warranty. The "Sovereign LORD" alone is "my strong deliverer" (Psalm 140:7). Everybody else will wear out. They may pull us out of that pit and even hang around a while to push us away when we try to get right back in it. But eventually their backs will give out. And when they do, we're liable to be mad at them. In fact, we might not speak to them for years. They let us down.

A dear sister in Christ came to me grieving about the loss of a friendship. She described how her friend had been there for her through a difficult time. In fact, she'd never have made it without her. Her friend listened to her. Said she'd been there herself. She could relate and give great advice. They'd talked for hours. Gotten so tight. She'd become the closest confidante my sister in Christ had ever had.

Over time her friend seemed a little less attentive. Less warm. Less patient. Or was she just imagining things? After all, she was still polite. Then she took longer to return her calls. She'd hear that her friend was doing things they used to do with someone else. It hurt her feelings. She tried to talk to her about it. Her friend hugged her and said all was well and she loved her. I have no doubt she did. She just couldn't keep carrying her. Before long, she quit calling altogether.

Does this scenario sound familiar? If you can't relate, I can relate enough for both of us. And from both sides. I'm sure I've worn people out, and I've been worn out (we'll get to that in a minute). A fellow human may have initially pulled us out of a pit, but somewhere along the way, he or she accidentally sold us into the slavery of nearly debilitating disappointment. Even subtly encouraged yet unmet expectations can be devastating. When it happens, we reason that we might as well have stayed in the pit.

Tragically, countless relationships end exactly that way. Like a ravenous beast, they ultimately demand to be fed more than people have the emotional resources to give. Reasonable expectations cease to satisfy. The beast ties up both parties to a post of excessive responsibility. The ties are ordinarily too knotted and tangled to be sorted out rationally together. One person invariably cuts the rope before the other, leaving the remaining party feeling, in the words of William Dean Howells, "betrayed and baffled still."

I wouldn't for a minute minimize the pain of a relationship broken by unreasonable—or at the very least, unsustainable—expectations. I've knelt with too many weeping women at the altar of my church sanctuary only to learn that they needed prayer over feelings deeply hurt by someone sitting elsewhere in that room. We can sustain an offense from a friend or mentor that cuts as deep as any offense our own flesh and blood could render. When such a close and dependable relationship is injuriously severed, the knife penetrates to the exact depth we've invited them into our private lives. Indeed, one of the primary reasons we're so wounded is because the person knew what we were going through and still abandoned us.

What I'm about to say can be painful to hear, but I pray that God will use it toward someone's healing: sometimes a person abandons us not in spite of what we're going through, but directly because of it. They either ran out of answers or they ran out of energy and no longer had the wherewithal to go through it with us. If our helping friends actually did something that overtly wronged us, they bear responsibility before God for that. But if they wronged us only by running out of fuel and dropping out of the struggle, we might need to realize they've done all they felt they could humanly do and let them go without bitterness or anger.

You and I certainly don't want to be afraid of intimacy or shrink back from bearing our true estate with people. If we do that, we'll become as cold and hard as plastic and shelve ourselves from every purpose of our existence. (For starters, inauthentic people are ineffective people. For finishers, liberty cannot exist apart from transparency.) Human clay finds its moisture in relationships and will evaporate into dust without them. The problem comes when our idea of relationship becomes ownership—when we start thinking of the person who was willing to get into our mess with us as our personal trainer.

A few particularly faithful pit-pullers may genuinely try to hang with it for a while. For months. Even years. If they don't seem to complain much, maybe the process is feeding something unhealthy in them too. You may reason that at least they didn't sell you off into slavery. Oh, yes they did. The world has a name for this caravan: *codependency*. The only difference between the two scenarios is that, in this one, they jumped on the wagon to Egypt with you.

The autumn Melissa headed off to college, my buddy Bonita and I got the hair-brained idea to take golf lessons. With empty nests, we thought for sure we'd have time for a hobby. What idiots. And of all hobbies, why golf? I don't even like the game. It bores me. I don't like the outfits, and I certainly don't like the shoes. I nearly slid down on the linoleum every time I walked from the car into the kitchen. I don't like how you have to be quiet when other people swing. Personally, I like to cheer people on. And I don't think your body is supposed to twist that way either. It's not natural. Furthermore, it's hot outside in the summer. Especially three doors from Hades where I live. I hate golf.

But I like a few golfers, which is exactly how we got into this mess. I reckon we were trying to impress our husbands by thinking of something we could do together . . . like they were really going to shoot eighteen holes with us. Our men were wise enough to forego our offer for them to teach us to play. "How hard could it be?" we asked them. They knew what we know now: that neither marriage could have stood the strain. They dropped the cash for someone else to do it. A real, live golf pro.

I could tell the first day he didn't like us. I don't know what his problem was: perhaps he had a mean mother. Could we help it if the woman in the pro shop was still ringing up our new accessories when he was ready to start the lesson? In retrospect, I think he could tell by our brand-new golfing outfits that it was going to be a long day. My lower back kept itching and I finally realized I had forgotten to remove the price tag. I tried to yank it off without him seeing me, but I think he did anyway. I guess I wasn't very inconspicuous when

I stuck it in my golf shoe. I couldn't find a trash can. They don't have trash at that club.

"Do we bring our purses?"

He just stared at us, so we guessed not.

After finding a locker, we finally made our way to the golf cart for our quick zip to the putting green. I would just as soon have walked, but my shoes kept sticking in the grass. Wearing our best southern manners, Bonita and I could hardly get in the cart for insisting that the other take the front seat along-side the driver. "No, by all means, you sit up there!"

The pro curtly suggested that we sit down and get on our way. Then he hit a speed bump and our new sunglasses fell off. Looking back now, I suspect foul play. I'm nearly certain he was trying to throw *us* off. We nearly fell off all right, but not because of the speed bump. For some reason we got tickled and couldn't get a grip.

Particularly on the golf club. No matter how I tried, my hands just wouldn't line up that way. The man nearly gave me carpal tunnel. If he positioned my hands once on that handle, he did it a hundred times.

I'm not a stupid woman. Clearly golfing was outside my spiritual unction. Nevertheless, our spirits could not be damp-ened. Every time one of us hit the golf ball, the other one clapped. With boundless enthusiasm, I'd cheer, "Bonita, that was so good!" Then I'd putt and, good friend that she is, she'd return the affirmation. "Ah, Beth! Now, that was *really* good!"

Finally, the golf pro had heard enough. He darted his eyes back and forth between us almost like he was having a seizure. He waved his arms, displaying the unsightly sweat under the sleeves of his polo, and said, "Neither one of you is any good!"

That was my last golf lesson. It's a shame, I know, but who has the patience for a golf pro who obviously overlooks his morning devotionals? I tried to remind myself to pray for his mother.

That day when I drove away from the course, an eighteen-wheeler pulled in with a flatbed stacked to the sky with palettes of grass. Keith suggested they were mending the course.

Sometimes we latch onto someone for dear life who is no better off than we are. I believe strongly in support groups, but a support group alone will never get us out of a pit. Somebody in that group better be on the upside looking in. Preferably way up. Otherwise we're liable to keep cheering back and forth, "That was so good!" when in reality, none of us is doing well. If we keep patting each other on our broken backs, how will they ever mend? Christ asked the question more effectively in Luke 6:39: "Can the blind guide the blind? Shall they not both fall into a pit?" (ASV).

Need to come up for air? Okay, let's switch sides for a minute. Not only has each of us searched for a human deliverer, we've also tried to become a deliverer to someone else. I could offer an embarrassing number of personal examples, but I'll settle for one.

A couple of years ago a pit-dwelling loved one (not my husband or daughters) charged me with gallivanting all over the country to help others but not caring about her. The deeper she sunk in her pit, the deeper she became buried in her resentment.

Her accusation that I didn't care couldn't have been further from the truth. I loved her dearly. Deep within my heart, however, I couldn't deny that sometimes getting through to people to whom you're not so closely related can be substantially easier. And, to be honest, more pleasant. Face it. You can't walk away from someone you love nearly as cleanly.

Her resentment cut me to the quick. I had tried countless times to help, but I'd never thrown myself into her plight no holds barred. I'd never given her everything I had. I made a decision to do whatever it took to turn this woman around. Two months later we were both in shambles. She was mad at me and I was mad at her. Not speaking, as a matter of fact. I am thankful that we got over it, but the experience settled something that had always nagged at me: even if we are unselfish and undistracted enough to give another person our all for an indefinite period of time, can we save them from themselves? I don't think so.

Does this mean we should not get involved with hurting people? Not at all! We may be hopelessly inadequate as deliverers for one another, but never think for a moment we can't be used of God to affect profound change in someone's life.

That's the primary reason He leaves us here on Planet Earth after our citizenship has transferred to heaven.

We can have a tremendous impact over a life in the pit. First of all, we can impact pit-dwellers by example. We can show them that living outside the pit is possible by living that way ourselves. If living outside of pits is impossible, the whole concept remains celebratory theology at best and pitifully poor reality.

Second, we can impact pit-dwellers by prayer. Second Corinthians 1:10–11 adds a vital tag to Paul's testimony I quoted earlier concerning God's past, present, and future deliverance of His children: "On him we have set our hope that he will continue to deliver us as *you help us by your prayers*" (emphasis mine). We have a God-given invitation—if not responsibility—to join the process of someone's divine deliverance from peril or pit. When deliverance happens, the payoff is glorious.

Third, we can impact pit-dwellers by encouragement. Hebrews 3:13 calls us to "encourage one another daily . . . that none of you may be hardened by sin's deceitfulness." Satan has a tremendous investment in convincing a person that, with his or her track record, sustainable victory is impossible. That's a lie. Say so.

Fourth, we can impact pit-dwellers by doggedly directing them to Jesus. Like the men carrying the paralytic on the mat, do everything you can to "lay [the person] before Jesus" (Luke

5:18). All the while keep praying, encouraging, and living by example. And above all, keep telling her who the true Deliverer is. Keep pointing her toward the only One who will not let her down.

Fifth, to the degree that God has developed biblical wisdom in us, we can impact pit-dwellers through our advice and counsel. Particularly those who have been well trained to do so. I am a huge proponent of godly professional counseling. Got it myself, and I'm not sure where I'd be without it. I needed to share things with an unbiased party. With someone who was bound by professionalism to keep my confidences. With someone who'd heard stories like mine before. I hear things from time to time that baffle me beyond any advice I know to give. I simply have no mental file from which to pull a ready answer. Also, I must keep in mind that professional counseling is not my job.

Sometimes, however, it doesn't take a professional to give good advice. For example, a woman recently asked me if she could remain friends with the guy with whom she'd shared an extra-marital affair. "We were such good friends before." Yep, too good, I'd be willing to bet. My answer to her was a no-brainer. I didn't even need to pray about it. Forget it. Emotional ties can get tight enough to strangle a person long after physical intimacy concludes. When people repent, God removes their transgressions from them "as far as the east is from west" (Psalm 103:12). In situations like this woman's, the two transgressors are wisest to move likewise.

Many other answers are not as black and white as this one. Like at what point a spouse or a parent's emotional problems are severe enough to warrant separation. Or whether or not a person needs to be on medication. When someone brings me an issue way out of my league, I'm going to stay on her like a bird dog on point until she goes to counseling or seeks professional advice.

Even the best of godly counselors have to guard against their counselees setting them up as deliverers. Wise counselors know from experience they'll never live up to it. They also know they'd be nearly smothered to death if they tried. Yep, they'd be buried right there under the cell phone, beeper, Blackberry, letters, messages, and stacks of e-mail the counselee made use of in her relentless pursuit of her deliverer.

All of us were born with a natural tendency to attach ourselves to a savior and worship him. To see him high and lifted up. That's why it had better be Christ. We are safe with no other. Isaiah 43:11 says it succinctly: "I, even I, am the LORD, / and apart from me there is no savior."

No one else can handle the weight. They may try for a while. They may even like it for a while, because when someone looks up to you and depends on you, it can be heady. But sooner or later they will drop the rope. It's too much to carry.

Just like the men who lowered the paralytic through the roof of the home where Jesus was teaching, you finally have to let go of the rope and leave them with Jesus.

My buddy, Liz, and I have become pretty close through the taping of a dozen in-depth Bible studies. In fact, no one gets in my face like she does since she's my makeup artist. While finishing up my eyeliner before we taped a session a few days ago, she told me a story I can't resist telling you.

For many years she did the makeup and helped with the wardrobe for the annual Christmas pageant at her large, thriving church in Nashville. A choir of hundreds, authentic costumes, and extravagant sets made it quite a holiday event. The live animals, she explained, were a no-fail crowd pleaser. I could see why. Crowds don't tend to be as pleased with dead ones.

A few years ago she helped the guy playing Jesus get onto a large, stately stallion that had been positioned as usual just behind the curtain. The horse had been trained to await command before making his entrance—just as he'd done for several nights prior to this one. It was closing night and only seconds before the final scene where Jesus was supposed to ride out on the stage on a white horse just as Revelation 19 describes. Liz had placed the crown just right on the actor's head and taken great pains to make sure his robes were fashioned where they would flow dramatically behind him as the horse made its grand entrance. The scene had never failed to be a gloriously effective surprise she said. The crowd would always go wild.

All of a sudden the horse mistook a random loud noise as his command and off he went with a jolt onto center stage. Following suit, off the actor went as well—and, yes, with a jolt—right onto his backside in the middle of the platform. According to Liz, if his crown rolled an inch it rolled a mile. The packed house of four thousand all exclaimed in unison, "Ohhhhhhhh!"

Then, dead silence.

I have no idea what happened next. I lost control the second the rider did. I'll tell you what I told her once I pulled myself together. That's what happens when somebody tries to play Jesus. Sooner or later, they're coming off their high horse with a big, fat thud and that crown of theirs is going to roll until it spins to a stop right there at the feet of the One and Only. Needless to say, Liz had to re-do my eyeliner.

Maybe this chapter wasn't meant so much for you. I don't know. Maybe you can't think of a single time you made someone else responsible for your happiness . . . your wholeness . . . your fulfillment . . . your healing . . . your future.

But then again, maybe some of the fog has cleared on a relationship you believed at one time would be a deliverance of sorts for you. Instead, you were left disillusioned or disappointed when that person dropped the rope. Possibly devastated. Maybe you're beginning to see that this person wasn't being heartless and hateful. Just human. Didn't have what it took. Maybe you can allow God to bring you to the place to forgive that person for failing to be Jesus for you. Or maybe you should fire someone who still insists on trying. Maybe you—like me—can now forgive yourself for accidentally setting someone up for failure. Maybe that someone was you. And maybe both of us could just let Jesus be Jesus.

and
gave me
A
FIRM
PLACE to
STAND.

CHAPTER SIX

The Three Steps
Out of Your Pit

You can opt for God. Pitching every other plan, you can opt
for God. Thanks-but-no-thanks to every other deliverer,
you can opt for God. Without having a clue how it works, you
can opt for God. Without knowing the Old Testament from
the New, you can opt for God. Not just for His help, but for
His entire Person! The whole of God.

Oh, the wonder of the One who comes as Three! You
can opt for the *Father* who reigns as King over every intricate
detail in the universe and can micromanage a complicated life
like yours and mine. He who could halt the sun in the noon
sky if that's what your victory would take. He who could hurl
a star like a stone at your enemy should he get in His way.

You can opt for the *Son* who paid your debt in full, not
just to deliver you from earth to heaven when you die, but also
from pit to pavement while you live. In Him, you have the full
rights of sonship or daughtership, including the right to live
wildly in victory. Do you hear what I'm saying to you? I don't

care what kind of addiction you've had or what kind of places you've been, you have as much right to flourish in Christ's abundance as Billy Graham. He'd tell you the same thing. No head hanging is necessary unless Christ has crowned you with so much love and compassion that the weight of it sometimes bows your head in joyful worship and gratitude.

You can opt for the *Holy Spirit* who first hovered over the Genesis waters and brought order out of chaos. The One who infuses any willing vessel with throne-spilled power from the inside out. The One who enables a people bereft of holiness to be holy by His very presence within them. The One who—at our invitation—seeps like water under every closed door of our souls, filling each empty place with Himself until the flood rises and the door is swept from its hinges . . . and we are utterly open before Him.

The beautiful thing about opting for God is that you are opting for everything He brings. Because He is infinite, you will never reach the end of all He offers of Himself. Nothing on earth is like fully engaging with God. *Nothing.* Once you taste what I've tasted, nothing in the physical realm can touch it. Yet everything in the physical realm takes on brilliant color because of it. God's love is better than life. No one compares.

If you're willing to engage God as your deliverer from the pit, the full-throttle relationship you develop with Him will be the most glorious thing that has ever happened to you. Far more glorious than the deliverance itself. If you will take God up on what He offers so that you can live in victory, you will find thankfulness in your heart for every person who let you down. For ultimately, their failure set you up for this most ecstatic relationship you will ever experience.

If you're willing. Here comes the challenge. You may end up closing this book after what you read in the next fifteen seconds, but if you decide to take the challenge, beloved, you are on your way out of that pit. Here's the deal: God wants everything you've got. Uncontested priority. Every egg in one basket. All your weight on one limb. This very moment He has His fingers gripped on your chin, saying, "Right here, Child. Look right here. Don't look right or left. Stare straight into My face. I am your Deliverer. There is none like Me."

God will be your complete Deliverer or nothing at all. That's the one rule of divine rescue. This I can tell you from both Scripture and experience: God absolutely refuses to share His glory. Anyone who shares His position as deliverer in your life is sharing His glory. God won't stand for that. Sooner or later, someone's going to back off, and you don't want it to be God. He may use any number of people in your life—friends, a counselor, a family member, or fellow believer—to come alongside and encourage as part of His process. But He alone must deliver you . . . or you will never be free. How badly do you want out of that pit? And out of the cycle that draws you back into it? If you take on the tunnel-vision determination of Isaiah 50:7, you're headed out. "Therefore have I set my face like flint, / and I know I will not be put to shame."

With that one unwavering rule established, let's get busy. To get where we want to go, we need a comprehendible, biblical how-to. My intent in the pages of this book is to be a whole lot more than just spiritual. Please, Lord, I'm asking to be practical. A staggering number of our American churches never even tackle issues of sin, addiction, and defeat. You can get such a steady dose of "feel good" sermons that you actually start to feel pretty good about that pit you're in. That's not the goal. Soothing words can become just another drug we swallow to dull our pain.

On the other hand, other Christian environments that actually do exercise the courage to call sin a sin can sometimes be tiresomely long-winded on what's wrong with us and pitifully short on what to do about it. In a typical forty-minute message, thirty-five of them are often spent pounding on our transgressions and shortfalls and five on what to do about them. Never confuse getting bruised at church with getting better at church.

Picture attending a weekly weight-loss meeting and hearing, "You're too fat!" echoed throughout most of the session, followed by a succinct two-word wrap-up: "Lose weight!" You'd leave really encouraged, wouldn't you? Empowered for the task? Or drawn like a magnet to the Krispy Kreme drive-thru as you head home? Instead, and to their credit, countless weight-loss groups actually equip their participants for success, with victors candidly sharing what they discovered and those still in defeat standing on their tiptoes in a little ray of hope.

We Christians hold in our hands the incomparable Manual for life, bulging with instructions, reasons, and countless real, human examples to illustrate them. So why are we getting shown up all over the place? Painful irony. Many of us in sterner Christian circles have substituted equipping and getting equipped for weekly poundings. "You're too _____! Lose _____!" And they're probably right; we are too prideful, selfish, worldly, lustful, or whatever. And we do need to lose the root cause of those sins. But how do we lose it? We don't even know how we found it! If we're really convicted, we drag ourselves to the altar and tell God how sorry we are . . . *again*. And we do it for good reason. We are sorry. We're miserable. We know something has to change, but we've got so many issues, we don't know where to start. We don't even know who we are without them.

Still, we keep coming back to church because we figure we deserve, if not hell, at least a weekly beating. We then drag our battered souls to our cars feeling more defeated and condemned than when we arrived. If we've got a fancy enough vehicle (I don't), maybe it will purr when we turn the key, caress us with air conditioning, soothe us with music, and say something nice to us when we start the engine. Perhaps even give us directions to a good place to eat. For crying out loud, we have cars today that do a better job of telling us how to get where we want to go than the Christian community does.

I don't mean to sound cynical. I love the body of Christ deeply and, goodness knows, I love church. I've seen God perform miracles in so many lives, but I'm jealous for the tens of thousands, maybe hundreds of thousands, who still make their bed in a pit. Not one of us has to be left there. Every one of us who authentically calls Jesus Lord has the right and power to be victorious.

Contrary to popular practice, walking an aisle at church won't cut it, regardless of how much weeping and gnashing of teeth accompanies the walk. Don't get me wrong: I'm a big believer in dropping to my knees at a church altar and washing the invisible feet of Jesus with my tears. But if I return to my pew without any notion of how to go on from there, how will I ever escape that pit and discover any semblance of abundant life?

We need lasting answers that don't just target our behaviors. We need answers that tap the power of heaven and change the thoughts and feelings that drive those behaviors. It fills me with joy to know that God is giving voice to a growing number of teachers and preachers willing to trek the length and breadth of Scripture to help deeply stuck people find healing and form new habits. My hope is to follow suit and offer some practical page-to-the-pavement answers. We never know why, after a thousand voices, God suddenly causes one to pummel through the brick wall of our fixed minds and make sense to us. Give hope to us. Believing with all my heart that God manipulated your way into this message, I pray that this is your time. And this is my offering.

I believe the Bible proposes three steps out of the pit, and each involves your mouth:

- Cry out
- Confess
- Consent

Repeat these steps over and over until they fall effortlessly from your tongue and stitch their way into your gray matter. If you'll let them, they will be life to you. Let's take a look at each step. Our part of the process begins and extends in a very specific action described in Psalm 40, a portion of the Scripture that became the inspiration for this book:

> I waited patiently for the LORD;
>> he turned to me and heard my cry.
> He lifted me out of the slimy pit,
>> out of the mud and mire;
>> he set my feet on a rock
>> and gave me a firm place to stand.
> (Psalm 40:1–2)

In this passage, the pit-dweller's deliverance began with a cry. I'm not talking about tears. Yes, weeping may accompany this cry, but tears alone mean little. You've probably heard the saying: "Sentimentality is no indication of a warm heart. Nothing weeps more copiously than a chunk of ice." We can cry our eyes out over the pain of our situation and still refuse to change. Those kinds of tears often flow from our desperation for *God* to change and our frustration that He won't. If you're like me, sometimes you want Him to bend the rules for you and bless your disobedience or half-heartedness. Who doesn't want a shortcut? Don't we all want God to bless our marginal cooperation with mammoth results? A powerful anointing? A stunning harvest? An entirely altered family life? A final farewell to addiction?

His refusal to bend to our will may at first seem uncompassionate in light of all we've endured, but He's pushing for the best thing that will ever happen to us. God will never be codependent with you. He will never pat your broken back and say, "Who could blame you for all of this?" He wants you up on your feet, living abundantly, profoundly, effectively.

And it all begins with a cry. The kind the psalmist was talking about erupts from the deepest part of a person's soul as if his or her life depends on it. This cry from the depths makes its first good use of the pit, aiming the petition straight up those narrow walls to the throne of God as if shot like fireworks from the cylinder of a Roman candle. No random ear will do for this crier. He is aiming at the One who made all things, rules all things, and can change all things. The One who says nothing is impossible.

You will be hard pressed to find a more repetitive concept in Scripture than God's intervention coming as a direct response to someone crying out. Here are a few samples pulled like fish from a sea full of them:

- "For he will deliver the needy who cry out" (Psalm 72:12).
- "But he took note of their distress / when he heard their cry; for their sake he remembered his covenant / and out of his great love he relented" (Psalm 106:44–45).
- "The LORD is a refuge for the oppressed / a stronghold in times of trouble . . . he does not ignore the cry of the afflicted" (Psalm 9:9, 12).
- "I love the LORD, for he heard my voice; / he heard my cry for mercy. / Because he turned his ear to me, / I will call on him as long as I live" (Psalm 116:1–2).
- "To the LORD I cry aloud, / and he answers me from his holy hill" (Psalm 3:4).

Why does the process start with our cry? Why can't it just begin with our need? I mean, God is all knowing, for heaven's sake. He knows what we need before we ask Him, so why does He make us bother? Talk about a control freak!

Oh, come on; don't act so shocked. Be honest. Isn't that what we sometimes think? Mind you, God can do whatever He wants. He can run to the rescue of anyone, regardless of her awareness or acknowledgment of Him. No telling how many times He's done it for us and we simply never knew what trouble we avoided. However, Scripture proves that God more often waits until the challenge comes and the hurting cry out, just as we see in Exodus 3:7–8:

> The LORD said, "I have indeed seen the misery of my people in Egypt. I have heard them crying out because of their slave drivers, and I am concerned about their suffering. So I have come down to rescue them from the hand of the Egyptians and to bring them up out of that land into good and spacious land, a land flowing with milk and honey."

God is sovereign and has His own reasons for responding in the ways He does. But from what I can tell about Him, I think He usually waits for us to cry out so He can remove all doubt about who came to our rescue. If we never cried out and had no human to credit when the raging fires of our trials turned to embers, we'd likely chalk our deliverance up to circumstantial happenstance or saccharine philosophies like "Things have a way of working out, don't they?"

Things don't just work out. God works them out. Blessed is the one who knows it.

Further, God sees great advantage in awaiting our cry because He is unequivocally driven by relationship. Throughout your ascent out of that pit, never lose sight of the fact that God will forever be more interested in you knowing your Healer than experiencing His healing, and knowing your Deliverer than knowing your deliverance. The King of all creation wants to reveal Himself to you. His Highness is willing to come to us in our lowness. Our cries blow the lid off the cistern we're trapped in. They voice openness. Readiness. That's what God is after.

The kind of cry the psalmist describes can come either from the desperate (I *need* God and God alone) or the deliberate (I *want* God and God alone). Remember, we don't always have to wait until we're desperate. We can wise up enough to know how desperate we're going to be if we don't cry out immediately. Either approach, regardless of how it sounds to human ears, rises to the Throne with the volume of a foghorn in a shower stall. *Cry out.* Open your mouth, say, "God, help me!" and mean it. Not as a figure of speech. Not with half a heart. With everything you've got, look up and cry out. Bring heaven to a standstill. Get some attention.

Maybe you should do it like a guy I encountered not too long ago. I see the weirdest things in airports and on planes. A diehard people watcher, few things amuse me more than human idiosyncrasies. I guess I like the company, wad of weirdities that I am. Recently I sat in the middle seat of row six on a packed aircraft. Despite a jillion air miles I didn't get an upgrade, but I did get a seat in what I like to call the "getting classier" section just two rows south of the heavy veil. A thirty-something couple—attractive and knowing it—moved into the bulkhead seat right in front of me with an adorable toddler. Unless I don't know my head from a hole in the ground, the couple was successful and, boy, were they crisp in their Italian couture.

With all of our carry-ons in the overhead compartments, our tables in their upright and locked positions, our seatbacks forward, and our aisles clear, we taxied the runways so long I thought we might as well merge onto the freeway and drive. Finally the pilot told the flight attendants to be seated, as we'd been cleared for departure. We were just beginning that G-force feeling of the pedal-to-the-metal when the dashing young husband began to scream. And I mean *scream*.

I sat straight up in my chair, scrambling to see if he'd been stabbed and we'd been hijacked. His screams turned into bellowing booms I could make out even over the roar of the engine. "I hate flying! I hate it! Ohhhhhh! We're going to crash! Help me! Awwwwh! I hate this! I hate flying! Get me out of here!" On and on for five disturbing minutes.

Houston's bruised and swollen sky didn't help matters. We bounced all over the atmosphere looking for some smooth airspace, and with every jolt our fellow comrade belted out how he really felt about flying. My chin, along with those of my fellow passengers, had dropped to my seat belt. I knew nothing to do but pray for the poor guy, and for some reason I thought it might be more effective if I stretched forth my hand toward him like we sometimes do in particularly demonstrative prayer circles. You know, kind of Moses-like.

My gesture put the man sitting beside me over the edge, and he nearly hyperventilated, eyes darting back and forth, searching for an exit row. I think he thought I was putting a hex on the wailing dude and he was next.

The flight attendants were safely buckled out of sight, and when they finally emerged they appeared strangely oblivious. So did the toddler, but I chalk that up to Benadryl.

The demonstration ended as abruptly as it began. In retrospect, I wonder if he'd done it before. Not once did his young wife pat his arm and say a soothing word, nor did she ask the more pointed question: "What in heaven's name is wrong with you?" Instead, she glared at him unsympathetically with a look that said, "Are you almost done?"

Once we hit smooth air and the pilot turned off the fasten seat-belt sign, the husband wiped off his face, blew his nose, opened his novel, and acted as cheerful as a chimp for the remainder of the trip. The strongest thing he drank was a Diet Coke, but I can't say the same for the threesome right across from him. They never did get the color back in their faces.

Time flew by until the pilot asked the flight attendants to prepare the cabin for another on-time arrival. All of us in the three rows around Mr. Crybaby braced ourselves for an emotional landing. He was as tranquil as a cat in a patch of sunshine on a nippy day. Go figure.

But wait. Surely he'd be a bit embarrassed when we pulled up to the gate and got up to retrieve our carry-ons. Nope. He was completely comfortable in his beach-tanned skin. Acted like nothing on earth could be more natural than venting your fears when you have them. I bet he outlives the rest of us. If his wife lets him.

You can cry out like that. Loudly and demonstratively. Done it myself. Or you can do it face down on the ground making no sound at all, except for a groan you yourself can't even interpret. However you do it, just do it. And mean it. If you don't have it, if your throat is too parched from pain and your soul is too drained of the needed energy, ask God to give you what it takes. Cry out to the one and only God who can deliver you.

After you cry out, *confess*. Think sin, but then think wider. Though it's absolutely vital, confessing sin is not the only way we practice confession. Confession in its widest sense is our means of baring our hearts and souls before God. Confession is a way we agree with what God says about Himself and about us. Confession takes place every time you tell God how much you need Him. Tell Him what's on your mind. What kind of mess you're in. Who's in it with you. What's holding you back. What's on your heart. Who's on your case. Who's made you mad. Who's on your nerves. Who's broken your heart. Even if your first impulse is to think it's Him. As long as you can feel it, spill it. Psalm 145:18 says, "The LORD is near to all who call on him, / to all who call on him in truth."

All these things are confession, but whatever you do, don't overlook the unparalleled benefit of also confessing sin. Lay it right out there and hold your chin up while you do it. Let the light of God shine all over your sin so the two of you can sort it out and He can heal you. Everybody's got stuff to confess. We will never get so hyper-spiritual that we can authentically go days upon end without anything to confess, especially considering that God places our attitudes and motives on a level with our actions.

And while you're at it, don't forget to spit out sins of pride. Nothing contributes more to the length of our stay in the pit. Pride is the number one reason why a person who knows better remains reluctant to cry out to God. As you prepare for your ascent out of that pit, confess every sin of your own actions, words, or thoughts that you believe contribute to your defeat. In my own personal journey, God showed me that I'd never break the pit cycle if I didn't name every contribution I made to it and let Him deal with my self-destructive tendencies.

Even if you were thrown into your pit, search your heart to see if bitterness has taken root, if anger, lack of forgiveness, or coldness is building you a home down there under the ground. Examine your heart and see if, somewhere amid your loss of control, you sought to regain it with manipulation. Ask yourself if you use your love as a weapon. I had to ask myself every single one of these questions. Get as specific as you can, and when you think you've thought of everything, ask God if there is anything you're overlooking. This process may take days as God reveals things layer by layer. Keep responding when He does.

Not once does God convict us in order to make us feel like wretches. He's out to restore fellowship and to flip the breaker that shut off the power. Remember, God's pursuit is relationship. Confession is one way we talk back after He speaks. He initiates conversation through conviction, and we answer back through confession. Meanwhile, a miracle takes place. Heaven and earth, Immortal and mortal, Perfect and imperfect engage in dialogue. Conviction is a hand-delivered invitation to meet with God, and confession is an RSVP with immediate arrival.

As much as anything else, confession clears the path so the King of glory can come in. In order to get out of that pit and stay out, you and I need the unhindered power of the Holy Spirit. Unconfessed sin clogs the pipeline between God's throne and our vessel. If you hold nothing back, neither will God.

Confession, by the way, is incomplete until we actively accept God's certain forgiveness. Take a fresh look at 1 John 1:8–9: "If we claim to be without sin, we deceive ourselves and the truth is not in us. If we confess our sins, he is faithful and just and will forgive us our sins and purify us from all unrighteousness." And 1 John 3:21–22: "Dear friends, if our hearts do not condemn us, we have confidence before God and receive from him anything we ask, because we obey his commands and do what pleases him."

If our hearts do not condemn us. Our self-condemning hearts can't block our forgiveness, but they can keep us from feeling it. The result will be a twisted resignation to our own capacity to sin rather than confidence in God's capacity to restore us. The conversation God began through conviction doesn't end with our response of confession. It continues with God telling us through His Word that He forgives us (see 1 John 1:9; Micah 7:18) and completes the process in our appropriate and freeing response of grateful acceptance. We will never stay out of that pit until we believe all the way to the marrow of our bones that God has forgiven us. Take a look at King Hezekiah's words to his God in Isaiah 38:17:

> Surely it was for my benefit
> that I suffered such anguish.

In your love you kept me
from the pit of destruction;
you have put all my sins
behind your back.

Mine too! Music to my ears!

Here's how confession works: we lay all our sins at God's feet; He picks them up and throws *all* of them behind His back. In our Christian circles, we constantly talk about putting our past behind us. That's not good enough. It's too easy for us to turn around and pick it up again. We want our past behind God's back. That way we'll have to go through God to get back to it. Come let us reason together, beloved. Admit that you can't beat a deal like that.

The religious police warn us away from adopting that marrow-deep belief that we are forgiven. They're afraid God's complete removal of our debilitating load of guilt will make us feel so free that we'll throw caution to the winds and wander right back into that pit. Not so! In fact, the opposite is true. Our tendency to return over and over to the pit is driven by our deep conviction that we'll never be anything but trash. Never be anything but defeated. Not feeling forgiven is a far more powerful motivator to re-enter a pit than feeling forgiven will ever be. Few thinking people who feel squeaky clean for a change are compelled to dash right back into the mud. Almost always, those who jump back in never really believed what God said about them: I have put all your sins behind My back.

Cry out.

Confess.

We're considering three steps out of the pit. The third step is *consent*. I love this one. We're talking action verb acquiescence here. A glance at a definition of the noun form of *consent*, however, will shed some light on what this step is all about: "Compliance in or approval of what is done or proposed by another . . . agreement as to action or opinion . . . voluntary agreement."[1]

Consent is the most beautiful part of the process of getting out of a pit. There is no ambiguity about this step: it is definitely God's will. Determining God's will in so many other areas is less than certain. Like where He wants us to work. Where He wants us to move. Where He wants us to serve. Who He wants us to date. Whether or not we should marry. This is not one of those uncertain areas. This one's black and white. God wants you out of that pit. He wants you in victory. Out of defeat. Period. So all you have to do is *consent* to what He already wants.

Can you celebrate the simplicity of this step? Once you get the hang of it, I believe you will. First John 5:14–15 says, "This is the confidence we have in approaching God: that if we ask anything according to his will, he hears us. And if we know that he hears us—whatever we ask—we know that we have what we asked of him."

Beloved, God's will is for you to get out of that pit. If you will consent to the process, waiting upon God as He begins shifting, shoving, and rearranging things for your release, you can go ahead and start getting excited, because it *will* happen. Just as God promises in His Word. If you're ready to start actively consenting, I'm ready to tell you the most effective way to do it.

When I first introduced the three steps to you—cry out, confess, and consent—I told you that each of them involved your mouth. The ironic part of the process will be that you will most likely use your mouth before you use your faith. Here's why: for most of us who have failed over and over, our faith nearly disintegrated because somewhere along the way we confused faith in God with faith in ourselves. We've let ourselves down so many times that now we're nearly hopeless. In reality, however, we've given ourselves way too much credit. We think we're too much for God to handle. That the strength of our personal draw into the abyss exceeds the strength of God's draw to pull us out. Hence, we've rendered ourselves virtually faithless. The process can't just begin with our faith, because our faithlessness is our biggest problem. It's got to begin somewhere else.

Like with our mouths. We're going to learn to speak it out. And I don't mean mumbling under your breath. I want you to learn to cry out, confess, and consent using God's Word. And to do so, when at all possible, *out loud*. Volume is not the point. All you need is to have your own ears hear it. Why? I feel so strongly about this concept that I'm almost standing up at the keyboard to write it. Listen, beloved, "Faith comes from hearing, and hearing by the word of Christ" (Romans 10:17 NASB). Your faith will be built by hearing your own voice speak the words of Christ.

I have never come up with a more powerful way to pray than using Scripture. I will teach this method in appropriate contexts as long as I live, because I've seen such results from it. I don't always pray using Scripture, but when a serious situation arises, and particularly if it persists, I turn to God's Word every single time.

One reason Scripture is such a big help in prayer is because our challenges are often so overwhelming that we can't think of the right words to say. Another reason is because we can shift the burden of responsibility to God and His Word rather than ultimately crumbling under the weight of it ourselves. God's Word carries its own supernatural power. It's His very breath on the page that, when you voice it, you release into your own circumstances (see 2 Timothy 3:16).

I can feel totally hopeless over a situation, but when I begin to cry out, confess, and consent according to God's

Word, I soon feel the power of His Spirit start to fill me up from the tip of my feet to the top of my head. *Faith comes from hearing, and hearing by the word of Christ.* My faith returns and holy passion burns. God loves His Word; therefore, if God's Spirit that lives inside a believer has not been quenched by unconfessed sin, God responds every time He hears it spoken. Yes, faith is absolutely critical to the process, but you can't just sit in that pit until one day, out of the blue, you suddenly have the faith to get out. Let God use your mouth to build up your faith.

If you'll allow me, I'd like to give you a jump start so that you can get on with the process. At the back of the book you'll find Scriptures I've rewritten into prayers for you. You'll see that the Scripture Prayers don't have to be used word for word. What's vital is that we echo the principles of Scripture so our confidence can grow in the certainty that we're praying God's will.

You'll also see intervals where I encourage you to use your own words, pour out your own heart, and get very specific with God. You'll find a set of Scripture Prayers of the cry out/ confess/consent order for every day of the week. I'm asking you to use them over and over for as many weeks as necessary until you're off and running on your own with at least some of the concepts in play. Don't let up when you begin to feel better. Feeling better is not what we're after. The goal is freedom from the pit *for the rest of your life.*

On days when you feel down, overwhelmed, or discouraged, get to your Scripture Prayers all the faster. On the days when you want to do it least, do it most. Be onto the enemy's devices. He knows that if he can make you quit praying, he can make you stay in the pit. When the battle heats up, rest assured that you're worrying your enemy, and he's trying to distract or discredit you.

Also expect your flesh to balk. It's been in control a long time, and it's not going to give over easily. No matter how resistant you feel, practice your steps anyway. In fact, on the days you feel most defeated, most intimidated, consider doing several sets instead of one. Do the *crying out* segments together, then the *confessions*, then the *consents*. Whatever you do, don't quit. Show the enemy that if he messes with you, you'll just call out God's Word all the more. Nothing does him damage like the Sword of the Spirit.

I'm so proud of you for getting this far into this book. I want so badly for you to be victorious, and I know you can be. God's Word tells me you can. I also know that this system works. You have the power of the entire Godhead behind you. You have the Father's will, the Son's Word, and the Holy Spirit's way. What more could you need?

And, anyway, what do you have to lose except a pit? So start making some noise. I bet when all is said and done, you end up having a mouth as big as mine.

Praise the LORD, O my soul;
   all my inmost being, praise his holy name.
Praise the LORD, O my soul,
   and forget not all his benefits—
who forgives all your sins
   and heals all your diseases,
who redeems your life from the pit
   and crowns you with love and compassion,
who satisfies your desires with good things
   so that your youth is renewed like the
   eagle's.
(Psalm 103:1–5)

He *put* a NEW SONG in my mouth,

CHAPTER SEVEN

Waiting on God for Deliverance

God can deliver the most hardened criminal or the most hopeless addict in one second flat. With His eyes closed and His hands tied behind His back if He has a mind to. I know people who made themselves at home in a pit a hundred feet deep and a thousand days long and, seemingly without warning, experienced the instantaneous deliverance of God. One moment they were in the throes of habitual sin, and the next moment they were free as birds.

When that happens, I ask things like, "So you're saying that was it? You never fell back in? The whole nightmare was over? Is that what you're telling me?"

"Yep," they say. That's what they're telling me. And I believe them, mainly because I watch them like a hawk. Not because I'm skeptical. Well, sometimes I am. But mostly I watch them because I love a divine spectacle.

Carolina was one of those one-second wonders. Nicknamed for his South Carolina roots, he's been behind the bars of four American prisons in three different states and is currently serving a life sentence in Louisiana's Angola Prison. Amid thousands of hard-core inmates in what "has long been labeled the bloodiest prison in America," Carolina had an inordinate taste for violence that once earned him the reputation of one of Angola's most dangerous prisoners. Get a load of his story.

> Five years ago Carolina signed up for a three-day, in-prison ministry retreat. "I only went for the free-world food," he said. "I was plotting a very violent act and I figured this would be my last free-world food. To me, God was a fairy tale and anybody who believed in Him was a fairy."
>
> After a day at the retreat he was bored and getting anxious to leave. He became so agitated that the facilitator started to panic. And then suddenly: "With no preliminaries, no prayer, no blinding lights or trumpets, God just took the violence and bitterness right out of my heart," Carolina said.
>
> "I knew it was gone because I'd lived with it for forty-four years. I thought I'd lost my mind . . . Then I heard Jesus say, 'I love you.' It sounded like words from speakers at a concert.

In every joint of my body I felt Jesus say, 'I love you.' I started crying and I cried for two weeks. I hadn't cried since I was seven years old."[1]

And Jesus had him. Hook, line, and sinker. I have a feeling nobody calls him a fairy though.

Carolina may still be in a cell, but he's no longer in a pit. Exhilarating, isn't it? Nothing makes me happier than God showing off like that. I just returned from Anchorage, Alaska, where I spoke to several hundred inmates in a women's prison just outside the city. The service was voluntary, so only those who wanted to come were there. That's the way I like it, anyway.

Some of the younger inmates started sobbing the moment I opened my mouth, and they never stopped. They're still asking themselves how on earth they got into that mess. Others have checked in so many times they've quit asking. Drugs got most of them there, but I prayed for one woman incarcerated for murder. Many of them showed me pictures of their children, who were now lost to the state. My heart was broken over the hopeless look on some of their faces. Without Jesus, history reads just like prophecy. Far too many feel that the pattern of the past dictates an inevitable future. The fact that you already have means you always will.

I told this group the story in Acts of Paul and Silas in prison—how they were severely beaten and bound up in stocks, and how around midnight the two of them started praying and singing hymns. I don't think they burst into song because they felt like it. I'm not sure singing comes naturally to anyone who's just had the skin ripped off his back. I think they were trying like mad to take the edge off their agony by shifting their focus to Jesus. They weren't going to get any sleep anyway.

Turned out to be a good idea. I don't know if God clapped or stomped His feet to the music but "Suddenly there was such a violent earthquake that the foundations of the prison were shaken. At once all the prison doors flew open, and everybody's chains came loose" (16:26).

The prisoners didn't escape, but they surely did spring to life. I told the women I hoped something like that happens to them. Sometimes God can put you in a prison of sorts just to set you free. I left that night praying that God had caused an earthquake for a few, and that heaven heard some chains hit that old gym floor with a tinny clunk. Maybe God had marked His calendar for a little instantaneous deliverance. I never doubt He can. I'm utterly elated when He does. Those are the kinds of testimonies that launch our faith to the moon and bring our congregations to their feet, cheering madly. I love it. I love to hear it. I love to see it.

But I have not one time experienced it. Let me say that again. Not one time. Not even an instantaneous deliverance from something comparatively shallow like a mini-pit of some kind I dug with a soupspoon instead of a shovel. I won't even be heel deep, and still, I'll rarely walk away without a fight.

For example, a sudden season of fear may overtake me. Out of thin air, all at once I'll get a notion that something is up with one of my loved ones or that a close relationship is threatened in some way. Sometimes I'm right. Other times I made it up. I just don't know it yet. Depending on what kind of vain imaginations are circling like vultures in my brain, I'll begin to feel anxious, insecure, or intimidated. In my rational mind I may know the fear is unfounded. Even ridiculous. Still, at times I'll let it get to me until it has a grip on me.

I'm not a glutton for punishment. Goodness knows I volunteer for instant deliverance the second I realize I'm wigging. I try to pray and say all the right things, like, "Lord, starting today I never want to think that way about that situation (or person) again. Forgive me and free me of this in Jesus' name. I know You can deliver me. Please do. And, if I may humbly ask, right this second." And next thing you know, all those vain imaginations invade in my mind again. They're all I can think about. So God and I have to get back to work.

The process may last a few days, a few weeks, or I may hop from dot to dot in what feels like an eternal etcetera. But I can think of virtually nothing God has delivered me from overnight. When it comes to high maintenance, I put the "I" in high and the ten in maintenance. I've joked with my coworkers that when my life is over, the most fitting epitaph etched into my gravestone would probably be, "God got tired."

Just a few days ago I was frustrated with myself over an extended family relationship I'm not handling well. I should have more spiritual maturity than to feel some of the things I'm battling. It's just that I'm spent. Dog tired. No, come to think of it, I'm mad. I don't think the situation is going to change, so I may as well get a clue: God wants *me* to change. I want that too. I like this side of myself less than anyone could.

Haunted and hating it, I awakened before sunup that morning and headed out to the back porch where I have my morning prayer time. I do my best praying outside. There's just something about not having a roof between God and me. I realize He is as present indoors as out, but I love looking straight up into the morning stars and talking to their Maker and mine. After a while, just like clockwork, God orders them offstage and raises the curtain on the rising sun. Once again, the sun comes up on brand new mercies He's set aside just for me. Boy, am I going to need them.

I especially needed them that morning. Painfully aware of my shortcomings and having that nagging feeling that God was saying, "I didn't raise you to act like this," I didn't even wait for my coffee to drip. I'm not sure I closed the door behind me. I think my knees were already buckling when I stepped over the threshold. I sprawled out prostrate right then and there on the patio. (I have to put the dogs up when I'm that demonstrative. It upsets them and they sniff my hair a lot. I don't know why. I think to see if I'm dead.)

After I got up off the ground, I resumed a regular prayer time at my porch table and let God reassure me with His love and instruct me with His Word. It wasn't until later that I realized I had specks of gravel stuck on my forehead. I nearly laughed out loud. Some of us, especially yours truly, would be wise to start our day with our foreheads on the floor and live the rest of the day with the floor on our foreheads.

I'm telling you, God and I work hard together. Maybe you consume a fair amount of divine energy yourself and, if so, perhaps we could sift some mutual encouragement out of the aggravation of never doing anything easily. I've come to the elementary conclusion that, to God, *together* is the whole point of any process. Before man was created, God just said something and it happened. "Let there be light" and all. He could still do that. Sometimes still does. But you might notice that a lot of that instantaneous action ceased after man came along, and obviously on God-purpose. Suddenly God wasn't so sudden. Time became the vehicle for this wonderful thing called history. You could neither rush it nor slow it. All you could do was ride it. And, what a ride it was for all those who preceded us.

What a ride it is for us now. God etched history not on lands and nations but on human lives. Not on superhumans.

Not even on particularly impressive humans. God seems to summon the most faithless of all to faith. He's a magnet to weakness, perhaps the ultimate proof that opposites really do attract. History is told through the encounters and experiences of men and women God would call to know Him. To trust Him, often under nearly impossible circumstances. People prone to wander, prone to bruising, prone to doubting, prone to losing.

Think about it. God could have accomplished in an instant many of the things that He decided instead to hammer out over the tedium of years. Sarai could have felt Isaac kick lustily within her before the dust of Ur was off of Abram's sandals. God takes His own sweet time because sweet time is God's to take. Still, if man weren't around, I personally think He'd go back into the instant-action mode. Why wait if there's no one to wait with you? God created time for man. In fact, even the words "in the beginning" mark the tick of the first clock. The Trinity has no such bounds in the eternal state. A wait is time oriented and, therefore, primarily man oriented. Perhaps among a host of other reasons, I think God often ordains a wait because He purely enjoys the togetherness of it.

Recently one of our best friends got a staph infection and kissed death on the cheek so many times we still don't know how he kept from going home with it. His closest friends hovered at the door of ICU for days. We hadn't been together like that in years. Hadn't had time. Suddenly a life-and-death crisis came and we made time. *Relationship*. That's one of the best things that can come out of a waiting room. Even the faith in God that an intense wait demands is about relationship. God calls upon us to walk in faith because faith requires a partner to place it in.

Not long ago when I battled those confounded health problems, a loving coworker was a bit mystified over the distraction God had allowed in my life at such a very busy time. I know I didn't need to take up for Him, but I did anyway. "I think He missed me," I told her. She nodded, "I understand." And by the way she smiled I knew she'd experienced exactly what I was talking about. In the relatively smooth days preceding the health issue, I had still sought Him and served Him in one capacity or another virtually every day and, heaven knows, I still loved Him. But smooth living invariably, eventually, makes for sloppy spirituality. I want consuming fire to rage in my soul, and if it's got to come through fiery trial, so be it. I want Jesus. A lot of Him. And obviously, He wanted me. *All of me*.

The same is true for you. Maybe we could take it as a compliment. As we discussed in chapter six, God is driven by relationship. It takes two to tango, even out of a pit. His part is to lift you out. Your part is to hold on for dear life. That's the liberty tango.

Instantaneous deliverance is what most highly motivates some people to cleave to the side of Jesus. The stunning display of His power and majesty is enough to super-glue them together forever. Others of us, after experiencing instantaneous deliverance, are thankful for a while, but soon we go our own way, assuring God that we'll let Him know when we need Him again. You know the kind: *Don't call us. We'll call You.* That's how I'd probably be.

Now that I think of it, the fact that I can't remember ever experiencing an instantaneous deliverance may not mean it hasn't happened. It may indicate it didn't end up meaning enough to me to remember it. Listen, beloved. God does whatever works, whether instantaneous or a long process. Obviously, a process works best for me because, based on our history, God and I really get into it.

You too? Then we're in good company, because apparently God and the psalmist were into a process too. Take a good look at the first three words out of the psalmist's mouth in his testimony of deliverance from the pit.

I waited patiently for the LORD;
    he turned to me and heard my cry.
He lifted me out of the slimy pit,
    out of the mud and mire. (Psalm 40:1–2)

You don't have to wait—patiently or otherwise—for

instant deliverance. It just happens . . . like it did for Carolina.[2] Obviously it didn't happen that way for the writer of our psalm. He encountered the tick and tock of time between the petition and the fruition. If we approach God humbly for instantaneous deliverance, knowing good and well He can give it, yet He chooses instead to use the wagon of time, He's writing history with each ponderous turn of the wheel and you're riding shotgun. Good stories don't jump on a page. They toss and turn, ebb and flow, rise and fall, just like the heaving chest of Adam as God first breathed that soul into his brand new corpse. Life on Planet Earth can never be static. Even in his stillest state, man inhales and exhales, lifts up and lilts down.

The good news is we may have to wait for deliverance while the vehicle of time jolts and lurches, but we never have to wait on God Himself. Never have to wait to enjoy His Presence or be reassured of His love. If we're willing to take God at His Word, we can have any one of those relational delights instantly. The only wait is on seeing His work manifest in the physical realm, seeing our petition come to fruition.

Despite appearances, huge things happen as you wait upon the Lord to deliver you from that pit. They begin the moment you cry out. In fact, you can tell the process is well under way the moment you begin reversing the three characteristics of a pit. Remember them? You feel stuck, you can't stand up, you've lost your vision. When you are convinced that you're no longer hopelessly stuck (you proved that when you cried out), when you resume a standing position against the enemy (you did that when you began confessing truth and consenting to God), and you're regaining glimpses of vision (you realize God doesn't hate you nor is He, worse, oblivious to you), you're no longer in the dark of the deep. Until you're all the way out, you wait . . . but not the way English-speaking people like you and me define waiting.

As you read the psalmist's description of having "waited patiently for the LORD," don't get the idea that he sat around in the mire, sinking deeper every minute, telling God to take all the time He needed. The phrase "waited patiently" is translated from a single Hebrew word *qwh*, (pronounced *kaw-VAW*).[3] The same word is also used in Isaiah 64:3, where in reference to God, Isaiah writes, "For when you did awesome things that we did not expect, / you came down, and the mountains trembled before you."

Here, the Hebrew *qwh* is translated *expect*. *The Theological Dictionary of the Old Testament* speaks of the "goal-oriented character of the verb *qwh*."[4] The psalmist didn't sit in the pit and twiddle his muddy thumbs until God delivered him. He postured himself in absolute expectation. He had a goal, and his shoulders would not slump till he saw it fulfilled. His Deliverer was coming and, on His way, fighting battles and blazing paths somewhere beyond the psalmist's gaze.

Never fear that God is not at work while you wait. He's doing what no one else can. Get a load of Isaiah 64:4:

Since the beginning of the world
men have not heard nor perceived by the
ear,
nor has the eye seen any God besides You,
who acts for the one who waits for Him."
(NKJV)

If your eyes could only see how God is moving all those chess pieces around the board for maximum impact, it would blow your mind. He's up to something big that affects not only you, but those around you. He's also after those around you. Furthermore, He's not just interested in impacting the present. He is the One "who is, and who was, and who is to come, the Almighty" (Revelation 1:8). Within every "is," God is mindful of what "was" and what "is to come" and He intends to show Himself mighty in all of the above. One thing is certain: you can't accuse God of being shortsighted.

God places a tremendous premium on lineage in His Word, and also on the influence one generation has on the next. To make the point, in fact, Scripture tells us that a thousand generations can reap the benefits of God's gracious favor over one who loved Him and followed Him feverishly and obediently (Exodus 20:6). God has the capacity to mark your entire family line—be it physical descendants or spiritual descendants you mentored in the faith—with blessing and with the highest privilege of bringing Him glory. God's agenda is not just to deliver you from the pit. His preeminent aim is to bring Himself fame, and you are one way He has chosen to do it. Anticipate it.

The word *qwh* is also translated "wait" in Psalm 130, where the eager expectation is beautifully clear from the context:

> Out of the depths I cry to you, O LORD;
> O Lord, hear my voice.
>> Let your ears be attentive
>> to my cry for mercy.
> If you, O LORD, kept a record of sins,
>> O lord, who could stand?
> But with you there is forgiveness;
>> therefore you are feared.
> I wait for the LORD, my soul waits,
>> and in his word I put my hope.
> My soul waits for the Lord
>> more than watchmen wait for the
> morning,
>> more than watchmen wait for the morning.
> (vv. 1–6)

The psalmist watched for God like a civil watchman gazing at the horizon from atop the city wall, waiting for the victorious King to come into full view. According to the Lexical

Aids of *The Complete Word Study Old Testament*, the Hebrew word *qwh* means "to lie in wait for someone . . . to expect, await, look for patiently, hope; to be confident, trust; to be enduring."[5] What does a watchman have to do with us? In God-terms, waiting means adopting a watchman's posture. His goal-orientation. His bird-seat. After we've cried out to the one and only true Deliverer, we are exhorted by Scripture to exercise unwavering and daily confidence that God is coming to our rescue. That means ceasing to make ourselves comfortable in that pit another day. Spiritually speaking, stand up and watch. Anticipate your absolute, inevitable deliverance.

As we watch and anticipate, we have the opportunity to practice one other part of the definition of *qwh*. As a matter of fact, it's my favorite part. *The Complete Word Study Old Testament* adds to the definition of the word, telling us it also means, "to bind together (by twisting)."[6] Let me help you picture what this means.

After a lifetime full of dysfunctional relationships and inevitably unmet expectations, motherhood somehow turned out to be everything I imagined it to be. More than I imagined it to be. Nothing had ever hit me with that kind of gale force. I'd been had by something my husband said wasn't even the size of an impressive striped bass but with about the same amount of hair. With her almost indiscernible infant breath, Amanda huffed and puffed and blew down the house I'd built around my heart.

Having foreseen and perfectly timed the opportunity, God wisely used my firstborn to make my getting well and becoming a whole person finally worth any amount of work it required. Sadly, I didn't like myself enough to do it just for me. Sadder still, I didn't trust God enough at that time to do it for Him. But He knew that I finally held something in my arms so precious and yet so emotionally vulnerable I'd do anything not to totally mess her up. I still would.

The stork dropped this surprise package on Keith and me when we'd barely been married ten months. The doctors had said I'd need surgery to conceive. They were wrong. I'm pretty sure God timed it early so my man and I would have a little extra incentive to stay together through tumultuous years.

Twenty-two years old and the first in my group of friends to be a mom, I didn't have a clue what to do with a toddler, so I did what came naturally to my sanguine personality. I played with her. We had a repertoire of games, but one was Amanda's favorite, hands down. It always came at the end of play time when I told her that Mommy needed to straighten up the house before Daddy got home. I'd take on a certain dead-give-away tone, pretending to heap a little guilt, and tell her not to worry. She could go right on playing while I got to work. That was code language for "climb on." She'd grin and act like she was going about her business, but when I turned my head, she'd throw her arms around my thigh and put both little feet on one of mine.

Her ten pink toenails stayed planted atop five of mine. Wherever I walked, she rode. I knew the game well, so I'd start putting dishes in the sink and clothes in the washer, pretending I was oblivious to the tiny tot I was dragging along on my leg.

Finally, I'd call her. "Amanda? Where'd you go? I can't find you anywhere! Answer your mother this second!" She'd giggle her head off.

Dragging her from room to room on my right foot, I'd look behind the furniture and in the closet, all the while calling her name. When she couldn't bear keeping the secret any more, she'd yell out, "I'm right here, silly Mommy! Look right down here!" I'd glance down with pretend shock and jump and squeal like she'd scared me half to death. We'd both laugh ourselves silly . . . then we'd do it again the next day.

When Melissa came along shortly afterward, her big sister taught her the game the moment she was barely old enough to stand up and hang on. I'd walk all over the house with those two munchkins atop my aching feet. By the time I was supposed to call out their names, I was out of breath.

That's the picture of *qwh*. While you wait for God to work and to manifest your sure deliverance, you wrap yourself around Him as tightly as you possibly can. Ask Him to make you more God-aware than you have ever been in your life. Bind yourself to Him with everything you've got so that you will ultimately—inevitably—go anywhere He does. Hang on for dear life and never let go. No matter how long it takes, He'll never run out of breath or stop to soak His aching feet. Pin yourself so close to Him you can almost hear Him whisper. His words will live in you and you will live in Him. God does not make His home in a pit. Bound to His holy robe, neither will you.

a
HYMN
of *praise*
to
OUR
GOD.

CHAPTER EIGHT

Make Up Your Mind

So how do you know when the wait is over and you're finally out of that pit? Two ways. Psalm 40:2 describes the first one:

> He lifted me out of the slimy pit,
> > out of the mud and mire;
> he set my feet on a rock
> > and gave me a firm place to stand.

One way you know you're out is when you realize after all the slip-sliding and sky diving you've done, your feet are finally planted on a rock, and you've got a firm place to stand. It means you've found a steady place where you can stand all the way up and rest your whole weight on your feet without fear of eventually discovering you're knee deep in new quicksand. Even if the mountains fall into the sea, you're secure. Even if the seas overtake the shores, you're not going anywhere. If earthly rulers fall and stock markets crash, your feet are steadfast. Knees needn't wobble. As long as you rest all your weight on that rock, you're not going to fall. Winds may blow and waters rise, but you will not lose ground. Praise His steadfast name, God is not a divine rug someone can pull out from under your feet.

Nor is He a fad. I remember when one of my neighbors realized I was in "religious" work after we'd enjoyed a very natural and amiable cul-de-sac relationship for several years. She already knew we were Christians, but somehow learning what I did for a living put her over the edge. Trust me, I didn't tell. Someone else squealed on me. My heart sank when she suddenly felt uncomfortable around me and needlessly scrambled for some kind of common ground for conversation. The conversations about our kids had worked well before, but her newfound knowledge of my work tricked her into thinking they were too trivial to talk about any more. I could see her mental Rolodex turning like a hamster on a wheel. As if a cartoon light bulb popped over her head, she all at once recalled a close relative and blurted out, "He had a religious spell, too, when he had that skin cancer."

God is unreasonably patient and merciful. He's there for every urgent need and any sudden spell, but an emergency room relationship with God is not the psalmist's idea of a firm place to stand. He's not a drive-thru drugstore. He is not just a temporary fix in an urgent situation, a fast way to get everyone to forgive us, or a good side to get on when we need Him to save our scrawny necks. God can hold your weight—the full emotional, spiritual, mental, and physical poundage of you—sixty seconds a minute, sixty minutes an hour, twenty-four hours a day, seven days a week, 365 days a year for the rest of your life.

I want to emphasize that phrase, *the rest of your life*. God is not just a firm place to stand. He's a firm place to stay. This book is not about getting out of the pit for a while. It's about getting out of the pit for good. And if that's what we want, we've got to do something absolutely crucial. We've got to make up our minds. The ground beneath our feet will be only as firm as our resolve. As long as we're wishy-washy, what's under us will be wishy-washy too. God *gives* us a firm place to stand, but we have to decide we want to take it. John 3:16 tells us that "God so loved the world that he gave his only Son," but He doesn't force anyone to take Him either. God is ever the Giver (see James 1:17) but, by His sovereign design, each individual gets to exercise the prerogative whether or not to be a taker.

We take the firm place He gives when we make up our minds and plant both our feet. That's exactly what the Hebrew word translated "firm" in Psalm 40:2 means. In another psalm it is used to characterize man's response to God. Psalm 78 speaks of a generation who:

> would put their trust in God
> and would not forget his deeds

but would keep his commands.
They would not be like their forefathers—
    a stubborn and rebellious generation,
    whose hearts were not loyal to God,
    whose spirits were not faithful to him.
(vv. 7–8)

You see that word "loyal"? It comes from the very same Hebrew word as "firm." God's complaint with the Israelites in Psalm 78 was their inability to make up their minds about Him. Were they with Him or not? Did they want a firm place to stand or an emergency room to visit? Like us, they wanted God when they were in trouble, but as soon as the pressure let up, they wanted to chart their own course and be their own boss. The momentary revelry of their rebellion turned into terrible bouts of captivity and consequences. They experienced what we do: the slide into the pit is the only thrill ride. From that point on, a pit's just dirt.

At its very core, loyalty means a made-up mind. It means that certain questions are already answered before life asks them. Since it shares the same definition as "firm," "loyal" in Psalm 78 means to be "sure . . . certain . . . ready . . . prepared . . . determined." It means we've settled some things in advance of the inevitable temptation to revert or destructively scratch a temporary itch. It means we don't wait until the heat of the moment to decide. You know what I'm talking about. A loyal spouse doesn't wait until someone flirts with her at work to decide if she's going to be faithful. She has already made the decision to stand by her man before a circumstance posed the question.

That's how God is about you. He's *firm*. He's *loyal*. He made up His mind about you before the foundation of the world. Regardless of who has betrayed you and what promises they didn't keep, God is firm in His commitment to you. Circumstances don't cause Him to rethink His position. Even if you, like me, have made multiple trips to the pit, His affection for you is unwavering. He's all yours if you want Him. The Rock is yours for the standing. Without hesitation God offers you a firm place to stand, but your feet are not firmly set in place until you've made up your own mind that's where you want to be. He will not force you to stand. And He most assuredly will not force you to stay.

I'll tell you why I'm hammering the point. Until you finally make up your mind that you're cleaving to God and calling upon His power from now until Hades freezes over, your feet are set upon a banana peel. You may stand while the wind is calm, but when the storm hits and the floodwaters rise, the undertow will leave you gulping for air. Case in point: my friend with a fierce drug dependency problem spoke to me recently of her extreme frustration with relapses and her confusion concerning her intermittent bouts of victory. She explained that she does "so well in between" crises. She gets along great as long as her ex-husband doesn't do something to remind her of rejection. She stays consistent as long as her kids don't have problems in school. She pedals along beautifully if she can pay her bills. She thinks that if she could rid herself of the problems that tempt her to drug use, she could stay on her feet.

The problem is, life on Planet Earth consists of one crisis after another. Beloved, this I promise you. Circumstances will offer unceasing invitations back to the pit. If our souls had no enemy, life on clay feet would still be hard. But the fact is we do have an enemy, and he formulates one scheme after another. He knows how to trip your switch. He finds your Achilles' heel, and that's where he aims his darts. And if he's anything at all, he's a great shot.

You can insulate yourself from the temptation for only so long. At some point you have to get out there, plant your own two feet upon that rock, and resist. Once, then twice. Ten times, then twenty-five. Thirty times, then fifty till your flesh submits and your enemy gives up on that front and quits. Sooner or later, relying on the power of Christ acting through you, you're going to have to face your foe and win. You can't just run from him and hide, because he'll keep showing up wherever you go.

Something happened recently to remind me of this fact. In our search for a peaceful corner of the West for writing, we intruded on bear country. My tiny writing cabin is nestled in the pine trees and aspens of Teton Forest where the tranquil beauty can be very deceiving. As long as those aspens have leaves, you've got a big threat in a bear suit. The only thing more dangerous than surprising and agitating a male grizzly is walking up on a protective female with a cub. I don't blame her. I mother just like that.

We've found paw prints with long claw marks close to the house countless times, and at other times even along the dirt driveway. We have one preserved on the back of our house where a bear must have braced himself to reach the limb of the nearby tree with his other paw. That print is right beside the bathroom window. Picture having a seat and minding your own business then glancing up nonchalantly to see the enormous head of a grizzly just on the other side of that thin pane of glass. A chill goes up my spine every time I let the dogs out before we go to bed only to have them bark their heads off at something they see in the dark. I decide they can go to sleep with full bladders.

Having a house in the wild means that I do things there that would seem insane in Houston. For instance, if I wheel up to the house alone, I honk the horn all the way up my driveway just in case something large and furry is lurking nearby. I'm a hiker, and even the locals tell me they never venture back into the woods without bear spray. I've never gotten used to it, but I can be prepared or be a fool.

Recently we had a change of scenery. I'm more of a mountain girl than a beach bunny, but Keith wanted to take a fishing trip on a small sliver of an island in Florida that has a reputation for great fishing. He took Melissa and me along, promising that I'd be able to write like a dream. It would be like taking candy from a baby. What could be more relaxing, right?

Our first sign of trouble should have been the tropical storm we followed onto the island. It left the pond on one side of our rented house swollen with water. Brackish water, my husband called it. Perhaps you can imagine the kinds of things that went through my head when Melissa yelled from the second-story porch, "There's a gator in the pond!" Great. Bears in Wyoming. Gators in Florida. Well, there you have it. Wherever you go, there's a foe.

Hurricanes in Houston. Tornadoes in Kansas. Earthquakes in California. Avalanches in Everest. Tsunamis in Asia. Welcome to life on our planet. The same gravity that sticks our feet to the floor throws curve balls through our air. One day we're well. The next day we're sick. At Christmas we get a bonus. In January we're in debt. If your victory depends on the right circumstances, you may as well wave the white flag and surrender to defeat. Just go ahead and take that snort. Gulp that fourth gin and tonic. Binge and purge that pizza, a side of garlic bread, and half gallon of mint chocolate chip. Sleep with that jerk again. Eat, drink, and be miserable.

Or you could make up your mind that you're in with

God, standing upon that rock, for the rest of your days. The apostle Paul called it being found in Christ (see Philippians 3:9). No matter how long it's been since you've seen me, He is where you can find me. Whether my health flourishes or fails, that's where I'll be. Richer or poorer, I've made up my mind. In the light of day or dark of night, find me in Christ. Spouse or not. Kids or not. Job or not. I've made up my mind.

When you've made that decision and given your heart, mind, and soul in all their fissured parts; and when you've given your past, present, and future "to him who is able to keep you from falling" (Jude 1:24); and when you know you're absolutely in, come what may . . . congratulations, Sweet Thing. You're out of the pit and your feet are on a rock.

Having a firm place to stand doesn't mean life isn't hard and temptations don't come. It doesn't mean you get everything right. It doesn't mean you don't sin, although you won't be able to wallow in it like you used to. It just means you've determined your position no matter what comes your way. You may sway back and forth. You may curl up in a ball or buck like a bronco. But you've decided where you're putting your feet. And once you're there, it's a mighty firm place to stand.

Don't get me wrong: we can live the other way and still be Christians, but we will live a tragic portion of our lives in ever-deepening misery and insecurity. Our feet will become like drill bits, spiraling us deeper and deeper until we sink so low into despair that we forget the scent of fresh air and the feeling of sunshine. If we've genuinely received Christ as our personal savior, our salvation is secure even if we live the rest of our lives driving in and out of a ditch. Eternal security is not the question. Earthly security is. Treating God like the divine drive-thru pharmacy where we can get a quick fix, we will live in a constant state of insecurity and uncertainty. Tums by day, Sominex by night.

With all due respect—and from one who has been there—it's time to make up your mind. Not only for all the reasons we've just discussed, but also for one other. You'd better brace yourself, because it's a whopper. I believe it may well be the biggest challenge of all, but I think you're up for it. Here's the pitiful truth, as well as I know how to tell it: there's nothing quite like trying to stay out of the pit while others close to you are still in it. I don't think I have to tell you that a whole family can take up residency in a deluxe-size pit with personalized compartments. So can a whole set of friends. Yep, right there on 105 South Pit Drive. Looks like a house. Acts like a pit. Make no mistake. A pit is an excellent place for a pileup.

Last year when Keith and I were coming home from mission work in Africa, we had a layover at London's Gatwick Airport and a near eternity to our next gate. After a ten-hour flight, our feet looked like four little pigs you could pop with a pin. So when we came upon a congested moving sidewalk, we decided we'd better forego the convenience and walk. Turned out to be a good decision. Just as we were walking parallel to the exit point of the moving sidewalk, a piece of luggage got stuck, and the woman behind it collapsed right on top of it. In a matter of seconds it caused a pileup that beat anything I'd ever seen on a football field. Suddenly something came over Keith. Like the Spirit of the Lord came over Samson. Trying to work quickly to keep people from getting hurt, he reached over and started pulling one person out with his right hand and another out with his left. He pulled at least eight people over that rail, each of them clearing it with the height of an Olympic jumper. I saw it with my own eyes . . . like watching a cartoon. All the while he was yelling, "Lizabeth! Find a button and push it! There's a button somewhere on this sidewalk!" Scrambling all over the place, I finally found it. With great drama and hopeful heroism, I pushed it, and the sidewalk came to a screeching halt.

The day was saved. Keith looked everyone over. Asked if he'd hurt anyone. If all were okay. They stared at him with eyes bugged, speechless and breathless but nodding. I think they thought they were looking square in the eyes of Clark Kent. For a minute there, I did too. Man, was I in love with him.

We didn't say a word all the way to the gate. After we took our seats on our next flight and buckled our belts, he looked over at me and said, "Did you see that?" Yep, I saw it all right.

Pileups happen. Especially in families. That's what happened to mine. That's what happened to Keith's. That's the nature of family. The ties are so close that the same cord that hangs one tangles all. They say alcoholism is a family disease, but it's not the only one. Both of my girls experienced some second-hand effects from my childhood victimization— Amanda battled outright fears, Melissa battled inward trust. And heaven knows my husband was affected just as I was by his family's losses.

Families pile up, but no matter who is at the bottom of it, no one is a lost cause. No one is too heavy to be pulled out. God delivers with "a mighty hand and an outstretched arm" (Deuteronomy 5:15). But He does it one person at a time. Remember, what He's after is relationship. What He wants takes place one on one. Nobody gets delivered on somebody else's coattail. Nobody gets out hanging onto somebody else's ankle. Jesus pulls each willing party out of the pit, one person at a time. And with His own scarred hand, by the way, just in case you think He doesn't get our pain.

If you're the first one who escapes a family pileup, you'd think your fellow pit-dwellers would be happy that at least you got out. You'd think your deliverance would give them hopes of their own, but for some reason that's often not the way it works. Usually when you get out of the pit, somebody in the family feels betrayed that you felt a change was necessary. They think it means you're saying something is wrong with the rest of them. Sometimes when a person decides to have a mind made up toward God and feet firmly set upon a rock, loyalty to Him is misinterpreted as disloyalty toward family.

Actually, nothing has the potential for greater positive impact in a close-knit group of people than when one decides to break tradition and pursue another level of wholeness. I am convinced that health can be even more contagious than infirmity. Until the breakthrough comes, however, and the Jesus-virus catches, you better glue your feet to that rock. The pressure to resume your old rank can be titanic.

When my beloved mother went home to be with the Lord, she was out of sorts with me. Had been for several years. I don't mean we lost touch. We never went a day without talking and hardly went a week without getting together. I never missed a single one of her cancer treatments, and she rarely missed a single one of my local speaking engagements. She had always been one of my favorite people in the whole world, and I'd spent much of my life trying to please her. Sadly, sometimes to the detriment of my marriage.

The conflict that emerged between us was not outright, but it was so strong that the undercurrent nearly swept me under. It was cold war. The Antarctic kind. I tried to talk to her about it, but she wouldn't admit that we had something between us. The rupture began when I wrote *Breaking Free*. The book was too serious for her. "Depressing," she said. I "used to be funnier."

I begged her to understand. Appealed to her sense of compassion. "Mom, people are hurting so badly. They don't need another motivational speech. They need freedom from countless abuses and addictions. They've been through all sorts of sufferings. They need to see the power of God's Word at work in a real, live fallible person. They need people like us to fess up to our pain."

Nope, she thought they just needed to get on with it like she did after some bad stuff happened to her in childhood.

I love my family of origin. I never wanted to do anything but honor them. I never wrote an ill word about them, but my mom felt strongly that my admission to having been abused by a person close to the family and turning out decidedly dysfunctional reflected negatively upon the entire family. God knows I was so crazy about my quirky and witty mom that it nearly broke my heart to lose her blessing. All my brothers and sisters and I courted her favor shamelessly. As her grave marker states, she was our "Queen of Everything," and in her mind, this little princess had messed up royally.

Lest you misunderstand, not for one second did I lose her love. I always knew that she loved me. She just tried to quit showing it as much, and she quit saying it entirely. If she meant to inflict some punishment, she certainly succeeded. As her cancer progressed, I knew the time was short, and I became sick of heart with the need to hear her say that she loved me. No matter how I tried to set up opportunities for her to tell me (e.g., something subtle like "I love you, Mom," with the kind of inflection that asked if she loved me too), she refrained. I could still cry over it.

One time I told her I wished I could trade places with her for a little while and take on her suffering. She looked back at me and responded, "Me too." I felt like I'd been hit squarely between the eyes with a stun gun. It's not that I didn't mean what I said. I did. What hurt me was the natural fact that a parent would carry almost any burden to keep it off her child. I wanted to yell, "I'm your baby! Remember me?" In reflection, I know that her poor body was so ill, so horrifically carved, and her mind so weary that she was not entirely responsible for some of the things she said ... or didn't say. God may likely let me be in a similar position one of these days, and we'll see just how sweet and affirming I feel like being.

I'm still crazy about my mother and have in my head an endless streaming video playing good times with her. No one made me laugh more. No one made me love my children more. I am confident that in her present and perfected state, she has forgiven my oversharing with you just as I must forgive her undersharing with me. In eternity our tongues will be loosed to say all the things we need to say. And perhaps I need to say more than she. You see, she may have said it all just before she died.

In my mom's last lucid hour God did something so tender and sweet for me. Maybe even a tad humorous. My mom looked at me with great urgency in her eyes and kept passionately saying something. By that time, however, we could no longer make out her words. Immediately I took it upon myself to assume she was trying to make peace with me. "Mom," I gushed with great emotion, "If you're trying to tell me you love me, I know that you do. I know that you never quit. I know that I just hurt your feelings. I love you so much, Mom, and you must rest assured that I know you love me!"

Like me, my siblings have a decidedly weird sense of humor. Later when I reveled in the firm conviction that my mom had finally said all the things I longed to hear, they told me she was talking to them. Several of us teased, cried, and elbowed one another saying,

"She was talking to *me*!"

"No, she wasn't! She was talking to *me*!"

"*I* was her favorite!"

"No, *I* was! She told it herself! Didn't you hear what she said? It was as plain as day!"

Each of us decided that her final words were everything we needed to hear from our mother. Rarely one to mince words, we know beyond a doubt that she will one day set us straight. In all likelihood, what she really said will turn out to be something like, "Could you guys back off and give me a little space? God's coming and you're in His way!" But until then, if it's all the same to you, we'll each think what we want.

Despite the cheesy picture decking the front of the Christmas card (yes, we send out those cards too), no family is perfect, and perhaps none less so than the one that tries to convince us it is. At the Moore home, we've given that up.

We're not cynical though, because we know as well as anyone could that entire families can be changed. I've seen it for myself. I am currently watching it happen in my own family of origin, but what has already happened in Keith's is nothing less than stunning. He and I have asked God to chase down every member of our extended families and make them His own. To heal any brokenness with His love and make every life matter. We've asked Him for such a mark on our family line that no generation will be without lovers of His Word, teachers of His truth, and followers of His way—right up to the very return of Christ.

If I were a wagering woman, I'd have placed my money on this happening in my family first, but the chase God has placed on Keith's has been relentless. We really never expected to see with our own human eyes much of the change we requested from God in our family lines. We expected to die seeing it in the distance and believing it all the same. Instead, it is happening right under our noses. (Of course, there's a lot of room under mine.)

Was it worth it? Was it worth not just accepting the family status quo but believing God for a better way? A healthier way? Was it worth being misunderstood? Was it worth being told you think you're better than them? Is it really possible to still treasure what you love most about your family's ways but exercise the prerogative to dump what you don't? You bet it is. Little by little we watched family resentment turn into at least a hint of respect, and at most a holy jealousy to have for themselves what we had found.

Sometimes the biggest favor you could ever do for your loved ones is the hardest. I wouldn't have told you that very private and painful story about my mom except that I need to earn enough credibility with you to make this next statement: nobody gets the right to keep you in a pit or to shame you for bailing. Not even your mama.

When God performs a dramatic deliverance in our lives, the nature of some of our closest relationships inevitably changes. The healthier we get, the more we realize how unhealthy we were. We find out quickly who has been a false Christ to us and how we may have been a false Christ to others. We find out where we've been motivated by guilt more than God. Or, for crying out loud, more than *love*.

Unhealthy relationships certainly don't develop only in pits of heinous sin. You can pile up in a pit you were innocently thrown into by something as tender and intimate as grief. I've known families that resented one of their members finally deciding that five or more years is long enough to deeply grieve that loss, and that it's time to move on. The betrayal is too much for the support heap, and the betrayer ends up losing not only the deceased one but the rest of the family as well. Sad, isn't it? Sad that in reality—despite our niceties—we don't always wish one another *well*.

Cooperating with God through painful relationship transitions may be the hardest work of all in our deliverance from the pit. Persevere with Him and trust Him—not just with your life, but also with their lives. You weren't doing them any favors by staying in the pit with them, despite what they say. Keep your feet upon that Rock no matter how plaintively beloved voices call from the pit and beg you to come quickly. Just as you waited upon God for your own deliverance, wait upon Him for theirs. Pray hard for them. Pray those Scriptures in the back of this book on their behalf. Love them lavishly, but as a Rock-dweller, not a fellow pit-dweller.

As you accomplish such an impressive feat, don't let the enemy tempt you into developing a prideful spirit because you're out and they're still in. Pride is the fastest track back. Through Christ alone "we have gained access by faith into this grace in which we now stand" (Romans 5:2). Your commitment to them from this new position has never been more vital.

Then again, not everybody is family; not every tie of the heartstring is God's will; and not every relationship needs to change. Some of them need to end. Just flat end. I don't know a nice way to say this. Some relationships won't survive your deliverance from the pit. And most of them don't need to. You discover that the pit was all you had in common, and that under different circumstances you wouldn't even have been drawn together. We can hope that this person is not your spouse. If it is, however, you start seeking God for a miracle just like Keith and I did. But if it's not a relationship God blesses, and not one His Word binds you to, it needs candid examination.

Start with the one you're most afraid of losing. Oh, I know. You think you can't live without that person, but that's not true. You can't live *with* him or her outside the pit. Infused with Christ's all surpassing power, you are so much tougher than you think you are.

I'm going to say it to you like I felt God say it to me: quit acting like a wimp. And quit the whining. It's depleting energy you need for the great escape. God has somewhere astounding to take you, and if you've got some people who won't let you go, you need to let them go.

You may ask, "Aren't we supposed to keep loving people no matter how messed up they are?" Absolutely, and sometimes letting go of them is the most loving thing we can do. If the person was unhealthy for you, it's highly likely that you were equally unhealthy for him or her. In no way do I mean to minimize the difficulty of walking away from some destructive relationships, but if all we do is focus on the hardship, we'll never get out of the mud. Our disfigured sympathies will keep us knee deep in the mire and our love will turn into resentment.

Ask yourself something I've had to ask myself in my pursuit of freedom. Which of your relationships are fueled by genuine affection, and which are fueled by addiction? Or, at what point did one transition from the former to the latter? I don't know about you, but I've done exactly what the apostle Paul accused the Galatians of doing. I've started relationships in the spirit that somewhere along the way veered into the flesh (Galatians 3:3). Regardless of how we began, we can become as emotionally addicted to a relationship as to a substance.

Beware of anyone who tries to become indispensable to you. Who becomes the one to whom you repeatedly say, "You're the only person on earth I can possibly trust." If that's really true, then you're not getting out enough. In fact, I'd be willing to bet that he or she is the biggest reason you're not getting out. Boldly identify any "pusher" in your life, anyone who keeps feeding the unhealthy part of you because it feeds the unhealthy part of her. Or of him. Question an inability to be alone. Is it possible that God can't even get to you because of that person? As we near the end of this journey together, I beg you to let no one "love" you to death.

Be brave, beloved. Be brave! Do the hard thing. Let that person go if that's what God is telling you. Remember what Keith said to me? Good-bye is a necessary life skill. Exercise it with a confidence only God can give you and don't beat around the bush when you do it. Has He not commanded you? "Be strong and courageous. Do not be terrified; do not be discouraged, for the LORD your God will be with you wherever you go" (Joshua 1:9). Say goodbye to that pit once and

Many will *will* SEE and fear

CHAPTER NINE

Singing a New Song

You will have a new song in your mouth, a hymn of praise to your God. That's the second way you'll know you've waved goodbye to the pit. Right after the psalmist tells us that God sets us on the rock and gives us a firm place to stand, he tells us God gives us a new song: "He put a new song in my mouth, / a hymn of praise to our God" (Psalm 40:3).

Every one of us was born for song. Even the one who can't carry a tune in a bucket. Even the one who hasn't turned on his radio since the invention of the cell phone. Even the one who wouldn't mind church so much if it weren't for the singing. The one who came for a sermon, not all that getting up and down. The one who wonders why some people don't feel silly about how they act during the music at church. The one who just doesn't get it—and doesn't think she wants to.

It doesn't matter whether you have a beautiful voice or make mostly noise, you were born for song. And not just any kind of song. Your heart beats to the rhythm of a God-song, and your vocal chords were fashioned to give it volume. That's not to say other kinds of songs aren't wonderful and even medicinal to the soul at times, since music—not to be confused with lyric—is a gift from God to man. Most of the time I'm a praise-and-worship/Christian-contemporary-music girl, but every now and then I feel blessed and freed to throw something else into the mix. I was raised in Arkansas in a time of fifty/fifty integration where the black kids won us white kids over hands down with their music. Is it any wonder? Those were the days of The Temptations when "Papa was a rollin' stone and wherever he laid his hat was his home." I never recovered, which might explain why CeCe Winans is the reigning queen of my iPod.

If the weather is just right, Keith and I occasionally jump in my car, open the sunroof, throw our Motown's greatest hits in the CD player, hit the road, and sing like there's no tomorrow. I've thought a lot about something he said to me a few months ago while we drove around belting it with that CD. "Ain't Too Proud to Beg" was blaring from the speakers. Soul sound doesn't get better than that. I was dancing around as much as my seatbelt would let me, snapping my fingers, swaying back and forth. "Man, I love this song!" I exclaimed.

Keith responded with equal enthusiasm, "I love how you act when you hear it!" I realized that even a man married to a Bible teacher likes for his wife to have a little sass. Maybe *espe-*

cially a man married to a Bible teacher. I promised myself I'd remember that.

It's true. Music of all kinds can get to you. Even intoxicate you when you're not one iota the drinking kind. I found that out for myself a year or so ago. I was invited to speak at a gathering in Washington, D.C., and, since my firstborn had never been there, I grabbed her and took her along. We were invited to go to the symphony at the prestigious Kennedy Center with once-in-a-lifetime seats in a bird's-eye box. We put on our fanciest duds and mingled with some of Washington's finest as we made our way through the wide corridors to our coveted seats. I was so excited I could hardly hold myself together. The musicians were all tuning and practicing their own instruments, oblivious to the ones beside them as that marvelously untamed and indistinguishable sound filled the house. It was thrilling. The whole affair was just like something you'd see in the movies. Something Audrey Hepburn would have attended, dressed just so.

I tried to read my program, but none of the songs had normal titles like "Cheeseburger in Paradise" or "Did I Shave My Legs For This?" I wanted so much to lean toward the person sitting next to me, point at a selection, and say, "Oh, I can hardly wait for this piece!" The trouble was the person sitting next to me was Amanda, and she knew that my usual idea of "a piece" was a piece of fried chicken. So I sat on the edge of my seat and practiced my own well-honed skill: I people watched. And what a watch it was! I'd never been more impressed with people, nor had I ever been more certain they were equally impressed with themselves.

I wish I could tell you that I am an experienced patron of the arts but, truthfully, I'm not even an experienced patron of arts and crafts. I love music, books, movies, and theaters, but at my own unsophisticated level. That night Ellie May Clampett had gone to the symphony, and she was sitting in my seat and wearing my hair. I was just sorry Jethro hadn't come wearing Keith's duds.

Just before the clock struck the hour, the audience began to cheer, and many of them stood to their feet. I searched the stage for the conductor, but he was nowhere to be found. Noting my obvious confusion, our experienced friend who had accompanied us explained, "The first-chair violinist is making her entrance."

Then I saw her. She was a vision. Her hair was pulled back in a bun. Her long black skirt flowed like billows of dark, mysterious clouds as she made her way across the stage. She looked just like a ballerina to me. She seemed to waltz her way to her seat as the crowd welcomed her with great fanfare. I was spellbound. Every woman in the room wanted to be her. I hardly noticed the conductor's entrance. I couldn't take my eyes off the exquisite violinist in the first chair.

Most of the time I didn't know what song we were on. Nor could I appreciate the guest pianist introduced in the middle of the evening, but I knew he was special. The crowd went absolutely wild. He would play several bars (just in case you know even less about music than I do, that's a musical term, not a place of business) then throw his head back and swing his arm behind him with tremendous drama. You might be impressed to know that I *am* actually a patron of the Houston Livestock Show and Rodeo, and the way the guest pianist played wildly with one hand reminded me of some bull riders I'd seen. I tried to relate as best I could.

As we neared the end of the evening, the songs heightened in a crescendo almost unbearable to the soul. Beethoven came back from the dead, kidnapped my emotions, and held me captive until I felt like crying. The last note burst like fireworks, and the conductor's wide-stretched hands hung in the air for what seemed like minutes, as if they'd been caught on the tip of a huge treble clef.

For a few seconds nobody could breathe. Breaking the silence, the woman just in front of me stood up and began yelling at the top of her lungs, "Bravo! Bravo!" I was astounded. I mean, let's face it. We all know what the word means, but how many of us have ever been in a place where they actually used it? In my usual settings, we more often yell something like, "Whoop! There it is!" This was my maiden voyage into Bravoville, and I was bug eyed. Then one by one people throughout the audience stood and cheered. "Bravo! Bravo!" Finally everyone in the great house was on their feet clapping their hands raw, and I, right there with them, screamed, "Bravo! Bravo!"

In just minutes we made our way into the hallowed halls where every face shone with artistic satisfaction. Indeed, we felt more excellent for having come. As for me, I waltzed out of the Kennedy Center in my black dress just like the ballerina making her way to the first chair. I couldn't help myself. I was totally intoxicated. Throughout our fashionably late night dinner in D.C., I used sophisticated language befitting a ballerina who plays the violin in the first chair. I ate light. You can't play an instrument like that with a full stomach. I acted like I knew things I don't. I felt lofty. High.

Close to midnight Amanda and I fell in the pillowy beds of our beautiful hotel room and silently took in our evening. Suddenly something came over me. It was my old self. I looked at Amanda and in my characteristically country tone yelled, "What the heck was that?" We laughed until we cried. We rolled back and forth, kicking our legs in the air, sides splitting until we hollered with pain. Right about then, Cinderella turned back into the Ellie May, saddled her horse, and headed back to Texas.

As good as the symphony was, a God-song in the simplest man's soul is more than that. It's not just a moment. It's not

just an emotional intoxication. It's the unleashed anthem of a
freed soul. A song expresses something no amount of spoken
words can articulate. No amount of nonverbal affection can
demonstrate. Music is its own thing, especially when instruments and voices respond to the tap of the divine Conductor.
Nothing can take a song's place. If its outlet gets clogged, the
soul gets heavier and heavier.

And nothing on earth clogs the windpipe like the polluted
air of a pit.

Few of us think of ourselves as troupers. We see other
Christians display remarkable character as they endure difficult times, but I'm not sure we ever see it in ourselves even
when it's there. Think about how often you've tried to affirm
someone for his strength in a certain tribulation, and he
wouldn't take the compliment. He knows the fear he faces in
the night, just like we do. He is painfully well acquainted with
his own weakness when no one's looking, just like we are. I
don't believe many people think themselves strong. We can
hear countless sermons on joy through tribulation, but we're
not sure we've ever had the spiritual fortitude to do anything
but whine through ours.

But did we often have a song on our hearts? Or one ready
on our lips? I'm not talking about the unbroken melody of a
beautiful singing voice. I'm talking about an unstopped outlet
of frequent compulsory praise. Of a raptured spirit. Of a

Sabbathed soul. In the midst of our difficulty, could we still sing with liberty to our God? Even with tears streaming down our cheeks?

Beloved, a song of praise freely sung and spontaneously offered is one of the most blatant trademarks of joy in tribulation. You have not let that situation get to you entirely and bury you in a pit until you've lost your God-song. Likewise, you know you're out of that pit when not only have your old songs returned but something fresh has happened. God has put a new song in your mouth. A brand-new hymn of praise to your God.

Having a new song in our mouths doesn't mean we're completely out of the pain that caused our pit or the pain that our pit caused. It doesn't even mean, if ours was a pit of sin, that all the consequences are necessarily behind us. It just means we're no longer stuck. No longer defeated. No longer caked in mud. Our vision is returning. Hints of creativity are reemerging. It's a new day, God doesn't hate us after all, and we can't help but praise. The wind is blowing in our faces once again and once more hope springs eternal.

I remember vividly every detail in my ascent from the worst pit of my life. I was driving home by myself from church on a winter night ablaze with brilliant stars, still in acute emotional pain from the situation I'd been in. Singing at the top of my lungs with the praise music blaring from my car speakers, I slid back my sunroof and screamed over and over, "I am free!" I was a long way from being out of pain but, make no mistake, I was out of that pit, and I knew—I absolutely *knew*—I was not going back.

Having a new song in our mouths doesn't necessarily mean we've learned three verses to a brand-new hymn replete with a chorus we've never heard before. It could happen that way. You could come out of a season of difficulty where a new Christian contemporary song or a praise and worship chorus becomes the expression of a fresh wave of love and awareness of Christ. Sometimes during worship at my church when the band begins a song that holds significance to me, I want to glance up toward heaven and say to Jesus, "They're playing our song."

When that happens it's a wonderful moment, but it's not what the psalmist means. He means that a whole new level of praise begins to erupt from a delivered soul. It's as if a lid pops off of an undiscovered canyon somewhere deep inside, and a dam of living water breaks, rinses, and fills it. A testimony of God's goodness springs from the well to the lips. Music comes alive and suddenly puts words to what you feel. You have a song on your heart that can't help but find its way—in various words and melodies—to your mouth. It must have been a fate worse than death for the psalmist to realize he'd lost his love of song. His expression of praise. After all, a song is what gave the psalmist (or song-ist) his name.

To some degree we're all psalmists. We all need song.

Music is as eternal as the Holy Trinity, ever attempting to fill God's boundless space with infinite echoes of majesty. The Father, Son, and Holy Spirit were surely the originators and trio emeritus of three-part harmony. According to Holy Writ, they apparently considered that something as marvelous and miraculous as the creation of Planet Earth needed accompaniment. Since each member of the Trinity would be busy doing the actual work, they shared the gift of song with others who would in turn play the divine score on perfect cue. Hear it for yourself in God's soliloquy to Job.

> Where were you when I laid the earth's
> foundation?
> Tell me, if you understand.
> Who marked off its dimensions? Surely you
> know!
> Who stretched a measuring line across it?
> On what were its footing set,
> or who laid its cornerstone—
> while the morning stars sang together
> and all the angels shouted for joy?
> (Job 38:4–7)

Can you imagine it? If music on earthly instruments and human tongues covers our arms with chill bumps, what

---

does music sound like at the portals of heaven? I think God opened one of my buddy's ears to that divine dimension for a few minutes once. Carrie McDonnall had suffered something few of us on this earth will ever experience. She was the solitary survivor of a spray of hateful gunfire opened upon the car that carried her and four other Christian relief workers on the streets of Iraq. Not only was she left without her precious husband of twenty-two months. She was left with a body riddled by bullets.

As I sat next to her bed in that hospital room, I knew I had never been beside a soul that had been through more. The whole day was surreal. I know this sounds weird but, as we talked, it was as if I could see Scripture hand-written by God on the walls. He seemed to transport that sterile, blank hospital room to a secret place behind the Veil for the briefest moment. Though her body was horribly broken, Carrie's words to me were seamlessly lucid and rational. As she described the horror of what she'd seen and experienced, she also described the miraculous. Among the wonders God graciously shared with His suffering young servant, He seemed to open her ears for a time to hear the music of heaven.

I don't know exactly what that song was all about. Maybe she got to hear her husband David's homecoming song. Or maybe it was a pilgrim psalm to encourage her to press on right here on this earth. Then again, maybe it was a song to help her offer what at that moment would probably have been a sacrifice of praise. Whatever the occasion for the music, Carrie testified that it was like nothing her ears had ever heard. She described a choir of countless voices, but my favorite part of her account was that she heard one set of harmony in one ear and another totally distinguishable set in the other. How gloriously odd of God! Perhaps when we get to heaven, our two immortalized ears will be able to hear and lucidly process two different things at once.

The songs of heaven are unceasingly sung. Unlike Carrie, most of us can't hear them simply because God has not unstopped our ears. Nevertheless, you can know they're being sung and—here's the best part for our present purposes—never more vividly than when a person like you or like me is being delivered.

Please sit up a little, shake the numbness from your head, and pay some extra mind as you read something else that the psalmist testified to his God:

> You are my hiding place;
> you will protect me from trouble
> and surround me with songs of deliverance.
> (Psalm 32:7)

If that's true—and God Himself says it is—some of those very songs are playing right now. In fact, according to that Scripture, this whole book and every other one like it must be set to music we can't hear. If you've been in a pit, God wants nothing more for you than deliverance, and He has surrounded you with accompaniment on your journey out. Take it seriously. No, take it joyfully. Gloriously! Think of the most dramatic movie you've ever seen. Hear the haunting score of the battle saga *Glory*. The thrilling score of final victory in Tolkien's *The Return of the King*. Hear the football players in *Remember the Titans* singing in the locker room, "Ain't no mountain high enough."

Now, imagine something even better. Surely you don't think earthly movie producers and composers have anything on God. Every Oscar winning expression of music is a mere echo of the God in whose image the clay-footed composer was created. With all this in mind, can you possibly think that God would deliver you in your real-life drama engaging both heaven and Earth without powerful accompaniment? Without poundings of percussion in the fury? Without weeping violins in the melancholy? Without trumpets of God in the victory? Without instruments you've never seen and sounds you've never heard? Not on your life. The originator of surround sound, God chases you down with melody and hems you in with harmony until your raptured soul finds liberty and your aching feet find stability. Christ, the King, the Creator of the Universe, seeks and surrounds *you* with songs of deliverance.

Can you let that sink into your swollen soul? Can you allow yourself to feel that loved? That sought? That significant? Maybe you and I will get to hear the scores accompanying each of our seasons of deliverance when we get to heaven. Picture Him handing us a personalized CD with a victorious scene from the final battle depicted on the front of it. Maybe it portrays the moment a former pit-dweller like me actually won for a change.

But now that I think about it, I hope it won't be just a CD. It needs to be a DVD. Real drama happens to real flesh and blood, playing out on the stage of earth's own sod but narrated from heaven's viewpoint. We won't just hear the music; we'll see the movie. Surely all the best parts are held in heavenly archives that will be opened to us when we're there. Only this time, we'll get to see the whole picture: the raging war in the unseen realm that took place over our heads as the angels of light fought the angels of darkness. We'll see exactly where Jesus was and what He was doing while every event unfolded. We'll hear the voice of God commanding the elements to cooperate. Our bonds to disintegrate. And, after all our waiting, we'll get to know the exact moment when God yelled, "Now!" Or at least I think we will. Because our King is a drama King. If He holds the score that contains the songs of our deliverance, why wouldn't He also have the nonfiction movie that the songs were written for? After all, what's a score without a scene?

Until then, go ahead and sing by faith. I know one thing:
the music is playing. And who knows? Maybe our souls can
hear what our ears can't discern.

If you've got guts enough, you might even go ahead, kick
up a little dust, and dance. That's what my staff and I did a
few days ago. I was finishing up a meeting with my correspon-
dence assistant in the office at the end of our hall, writing a few
notes to beloved sisters I've never met. It was a little past noon,
and the rest of my staff was gathered in the front office waiting to go to lunch. Friday is usually a great day at the ministry,
but on this particular Friday God had outdone the routine.
Answered prayers and causes for praise had been rolling in all
morning like He was in the mood to show off.

Suddenly I heard music coming from that front office.
Music with a beat you could feel in your bones. Then I heard
the pounding of stomping feet. "They're dancing!" I said to
Nancy. "Let's go join them!" I didn't have to say it twice. She
jumped like a jack-in-the-box and nearly beat me down the
hall. Spontaneous praise dancing isn't an everyday kind of
thing at Living Proof Ministries, and I intended not to miss it.
We ran into the front office where we joined our sisters, and
all of us—Baptist, Methodist, and Lutheran for starters—
sang, praised, and danced to beat the band. (Yes, modestly and
appropriately, in case you're a stick in the mud.)

Most of the floor was empty since everyone else had gone
to lunch. But while we were in the throes of happy worship,

two women walked past the glass front of our reception area, looking for the insurance office next door I suppose. They stopped in their tracks and mouthed, "What are y'all doing?"

I opened the door and yelled over the music, "God's been extra good to us this morning delivering a ton of answered prayer. We're just celebrating! Sorry if we disturbed you!"

They laughed nervously, looked at us like we were crazy, and walked on. Maybe ran on. Undeterred, we danced on.

Seconds later, they were back in that hall walking through our office door with tears in their eyes. "Do you think you could pray for her?" one asked as she held the hand of the other. "She's really having a tough time."

"We'd be delighted." My staff and I laid hands on that precious unsuspecting young woman and called heaven down on her and all that concerned her. Christ met Lacey on the dance floor that day to the tune of somebody else's song. That's the way it works sometimes. It's contagious, you see.

> He put a new song in my mouth,
>> a hymn of praise to our God.
>> Many will see and fear
>> and put their trust in the LORD.
> (Psalm 40:3)

and
PUT THEIR
TRUST
in the
LORD.

—Psalm 40:1–3

CHAPTER TEN

Our Pit-Less Future

My boots were made for walking, so I'm rarely anxious for a journey to end. On the other hand, I've just found it's always better to call it a day early than to stay a day too late. Well, I stayed a day too late, and as punishment, as well as to keep my publisher from having an apoplectic fit, I get to write this last chapter from Seat 14F on a packed flight from Washington, D.C., to Chicago's overstuffed O'Hare International. Walking boots or not, I'm ready to get there.

We took off a tad late, so when we land, Keith, Melissa, and I will run like the wind (maybe more like a mild breeze on our rubber legs) to another terminal where we hope to board the last leg of our long trip home from South Africa. After a week and a half of conferences and AIDs ministry in Cape Town and Johannesburg, and then a few days on safari staring into a nighttime sky you can only see from the bottom of the globe, it's time to go home. Especially since the U.S. Department of Homeland Security just banned all liquids and gels from passenger carry-ons in view of recent terrorist threats.

I don't like whiners so I'll point out with a stiff—but pale—upper lip that, for now, the ban includes cosmetics. Which includes—let me take a deep breath—lipstick. For me that means leaving behind all eight tubes of varying shades of pink that I go virtually nowhere without and haven't since I was fourteen years old.

Go ahead and call me prissy. I don't care. I haven't slept in something like forty days and forty nights, nor can I any longer recall my last shower, as the folks sitting next to me can probably testify. The way I see it, my neighbors on the plane could deal with the way I smell if I just looked better. I'm not sure if it helped, but I forewent the coffee and ordered tomato juice instead, in hopes that it stains my lips.

An odd thing happened on my last day in Johannesburg, where we spent our final few hours in a giant shopping mall. I was minding my own business in the food court when a perfectly normal-looking woman at the Kentucky Fried counter said in a thick South African accent, "Excuse me, ma'am. Would you like for me to read your Tarot cards?"

I glanced down at her three kids gnawing the Colonel's original recipe off a handful of chicken legs and then back at her. I could easily have taken her for a soccer mom. There she stood, with the expression of someone who had just asked me if I'd like to sample some barbeque wieners with a toothpick. My jet-lagged brain was trying to play catch-up with my ears.

"Uh, no. No, thank you. No cards, please. I'm just here for some . . . [suddenly I couldn't think what I was there for] *fish*. Fried fish. Thank you anyway."

Melissa and I were stunned. "Is she a witch?" I whispered to my youngest. The woman did have a gray streak at the widow's peak of her jet-black updo. Melissa has yet to develop an eye for witches, so she didn't know. Somehow in our apologetics classes she and I both missed the part about how to respond to a Tarot card reader.

That's not to say we know nothing about the future, because we do. Before you and I close this book and call it a day, I thought you might want to know how it all turns out. After all, life leaves us in the dark about so many things. When we're little we think we know what we want to be when we grow up, but when we're grown, many of us no longer have a clue. We walk down an aisle and make promises "till death do us part" but God only knows who will part first. Our babies take their first steps across the floor just to get to us, but we have no idea where life will really take them. Or if they'll still like us when they get there. We're diagnosed with chronic diseases and coldly told the survival rates, but we have no clue where our number will fall in those statistics. We watch world news and squirm with the fresh realization that a sound mind isn't necessarily a requirement for becoming a world leader. We wonder how in heaven's name some maniac hasn't lost his mind and blown up the planet yet. We blow our hair dry and wonder if we're contributing to global warming. If we live long enough and stay plugged in enough, we end up asking the same question our grandparents and parents asked: *What's this world coming to?* And we shake our heads like no one has any idea.

God left a lot of questions unanswered—primarily, I imagine, because "without faith it is impossible to please God" (Hebrews 11:6). I think He also happens to like surprises. However, what this world is coming to is not unanswered. According to Revelation 21, earth as we know it will come to an end, and God will usher into existence a new heaven and new earth with properties beyond our wildest imagination.

Most folks agree that heaven is a better option than hell but, comparatively speaking, only a handful of Christians really anticipate their futures there. Face it. We're scared to death that it's going to be like our church services, only instead of getting out at noon, it will last an eternity. For the life of us, we can't picture how anything holy can possibly be lively. Let alone fun.

A few years ago I was studying the seventh chapter of Revelation for a series I was teaching, and God brought back to my mind a familiar Old Testament passage using the same metaphor as in the passage I had just read. A wonderful contrast jumped off the page at me and sent my imagination whirling. See it for yourself. The first passage refers to life on earth. The second refers to life in heaven.

Psalm 23:1–3 says:

> The LORD *is* my shepherd;
>> I shall not want.
> He makes me to lie down in green pastures;
>> He leads me beside the still waters.
> He restores my soul. (NKJV)

Revelation 7:17 says, "For the Lamb at the center of the throne will be their shepherd; he will lead them to springs of living water."

Get a load of that: Still waters on earth. Springs of living water in heaven. Compared to the white-water existence we'll have in heaven, here we're like toads perched on the lily pad of a stagnant pond. Despite our expectations, heaven is where all the action is. Our present existence, replete with every sunrise, sunset, season change, mountain range, forest glen, and foaming sea, is a mere shadow of an unthinkable reality. Get the idea out of your head that life in a perfected state has got to be a letdown. Our hearts and minds still need considerable healing as long as somewhere deep inside we still associate fun with sin. No matter what somebody led you to believe, sin is not where all the fun is. As good as life on earth can be at times, clinging to this ride is like refusing to get off the barge that takes you from the parking lot to the gates of Disneyland.

I dearly love a great ending, and you need to know that we get one. The Author of our faith knows how to finish it. As we wrap up this book on getting out of the pit, I want you to know what happens to the devil when all is said and done. It's such poetic justice. Revelation 20:1–3 describes it:

> Then I saw an angel coming down from heaven,
> having the key to the bottomless pit and a great
> chain in his hand. He laid hold of the dragon,
> that serpent of old, who is *the* Devil and Satan,
> and bound him for a thousand years; and he
> cast him into the bottomless pit, and shut him
> up, and set a seal on him. (NKJV)

There you have it. Before the Lord does away with Satan once and for all, He's going to give him a taste of the pit. It's the perfect plan, really. And sublimely scriptural. After all, long ago Psalm 7:15–16 promised that

> He who digs a hole and scoops it out
> falls into the pit he has made.
> The trouble he causes recoils on himself;
> his violence comes down on his own head.

In God's economy those who dig a pit for others will invariably fall into it themselves (see Psalm 57:6). God writes perfect endings. He can't help it. He's a wordsmith if you'll ever meet one. Every beginning will have a fitting ending. After all the dirt the prowling lion has gathered in his paws digging pits for us, he will eventually find himself caged in a pit. Maybe the reason his pit is so deep is because God is scooping it out until it reaches the total depth of all the ones the devil dug for us. By the time Satan looks at life from a bottomless pit, our feet will forever be firmly set upon a rock. The air will be clear. The view crystal. The fellowship sweet. And the sufferings of this present time won't even be worthy to compare to the glory revealed to us (see Romans 8:18). We'll ride raftless in rivers of living water then bask in the Son.

Until then, life on this battered earth will not be easy, but we never have to make another bed in the bottom of a pit. We'll still have bad days, mind you. I had one yesterday and drank my sorrows to the coffee-ground-speckled dregs of my Starbuck's cappuccino. As I shook the cup to see if anything was left, my eyes fell on the quote of a musician printed on the back. Here's what it said: "It's tragic that extremists co-opt the notion of God, and that hipsters and artists reject spirituality out of hand. I don't have a fixed idea of God. But I feel that it's us—the messed-up, the half-crazy, the burning, the questing—that need God, a lot more than the goody-two-shoes do."[1]

I don't know anything about this guy or his broader theology. I just know I've been completely messed up and more than half crazy. And right there in the worst of it, right there while I was waist deep in the pit for what seemed the thousandth time, Christ stretched out His mighty arm, reached into the depths, and said in a way I could finally hear, "Need a hand?"

He bids me "Rise up," and well He may, for I have long enough been lying among the pots of worldliness. He is risen, I am risen in Him, why then should I cleave unto the dust? From lower loves, desires, pursuits, and aspirations, I would rise towards Him . . . But Lord, how can a stone rise, how can a lump of clay come away from the horrible pit? O raise me, draw me. Thy grace can do it. Send forth Thy Holy Spirit to kindle sacred flames of love in my heart, and I will continue to rise until I leave life and time behind me, and indeed come away.[2]

"Rise up, my love, my fair one, and come away."
(Song of Songs 2:10 KJV)

ENDNOTES

Chapter Two

1. Spiros Zodhiates, ed., "Lexical Aids to the New Testament," *The Hebrew-Greek Key Word Study Bible*: #1923 (Chattanooga, TN: AMG Publishers, 1998), 1,621.
2. Greg Paul, *God in the Alley* (Colorado Springs: Shaw, 2004), 37.

Chapter Four

1. Kurt Richardson, *New American Commentary: James* (Nashville: Broadman and Holman, 1997), 80 (see both text and footnote number 69).

Chapter Six

1. *Merriam-Webster Collegiate Dictionary*, 10th ed., s.v. "consent."

Chapter Seven

1 Steve Carr, "Set Free in Angola Prison," *Decision*, June 2006, 8.
2. Ibid, 11.
3. Spiros Zodhiates, ed., "Lexical Aids to the Old Testament," *The Hebrew-Greek Key Word Study Bible*: #7747 (Chattanooga, TN: AMG Publishers, 1998), 1,548.

4. G. Johannes Botterweck, Helmer Ringgren, and Heinz-Josef Fabry, eds., *The Theological Dictionary of the Old Testament* (Grand Rapids, MI: Eerdmans), 568.

5. Spiros Zodhiates and Warren Baker, eds., *The Complete Word Study Old Testament*, #6960 (Chattanooga, TN: AMG Publishers, 1994), 2360.

6. Ibid.

Chapter Ten

1. Mike Doughty, *The Way I See It #158* (Starbucks Coffee Cup Series, 2006).

2. Charles Spurgeon, *Morning and Evening*, Morning, April 25 (Nashville, TN: Thomas Nelson, 1994).

Each day before you begin to cry out, confess, and consent, get in the habit of echoing Christ's approach in John 11:41b–42, where He said, "Father, I thank you that you have heard me. I knew that you always hear me." Nothing causes us to lose confidence like a season in the pit. In order to strengthen your confidence in God and in the welcome you have before His Throne, begin each day's Scripture segment by stating your absolute certainty that He hears you when you pray. Say something like this:

> Father, Your Son died and rose again to give me direct access to You. That means I can pray like He prayed. In His name, I thank You in advance that You always hear me. I know You are listening to me right now and that my prayers always matter.

Then proceed.

SUNDAY

CRY OUT

I call to You, Lord, who are worthy of praise, and I am saved from my enemies. The waves of death swirl about me; the torrents of destruction overwhelm me. The cords of the grave coil around me; the snares of death confront me. In my distress I call to You, Lord; I call out to my God. From Your temple You hear my voice; my cry comes to Your ears (2 Samuel 22:4–7). O, my Strength, come quickly to help me (Psalm 22:19b). Reach down from on high and take hold of me; draw me out of deep waters. Rescue me from my powerful enemy and from foes, who are too strong for me (Psalm 18:16–17). Bring me out into a spacious place; rescue me, Lord, because You delight in me (Psalm 18:19).

Add any of your own words . . .

CONFESS

Search me, O God, and know my heart; test me and know my anxious thoughts. See if there is any offensive way in me, and lead me in the way everlasting (Psalm 139:23, 24). [When applicable . . .] Father, I want to acknowledge my sin to you. I don't want to cover it up. I will confess my transgressions to you, Lord, and You will forgive the guilt of my sin (Psalm 32:5). I confess that You are my rock, my fortress, and my deliverer;

You are my rock, in whom I take refuge, my shield and the horn of my salvation. You are my stronghold, my refuge, and my savior—save me from anything that seeks to destroy me (2 Samuel 22:2–3).

Add any of your own words ...

CONSENT

You are my lamp, O Lord; You turn my darkness into light. With Your help I can advance against a troop; with You I can scale a wall. As for You, my Father, Your way is perfect; Your Word is flawless. You are a shield for all who take refuge in You. For who is God besides You? And who is the Rock except You? (2 Samuel 22:29–32). If You are for me, who can be against me? You did not spare Your own Son but gave Him up for me. How will You not also, along with Him, graciously give me all things? (Romans 8:31–32). You know the plans You have for me, O God. Plans to prosper me and not to harm me. Plans to give me a hope and a future (Jeremiah 29:11). Thank You, God, for Your willingness to lead me to triumph (2 Corinthians 2:14).

Add any of your own words ...

MONDAY

CRY OUT

To You I call, O Lord my Rock; I believe You will not turn a deaf ear to me. For if You remained silent, I would be like those who stay in the pit. Hear my cry for mercy as I call to you for help (Psalm 28:1–2). I call with all my heart; answer me, O Lord. I want to obey Your decrees. I call out to You; save me and with Your help I will keep Your statutes. Help me rise before dawn and cry for help; I have put my hope in Your Word (Psalm 119:145–147). Lift me out of this slimy pit, out of the mud and mire. Set my feet on a rock and give me a firm place to stand. Put a new song in my mouth, a hymn of praise to You, my God. Cause many to see and put their trust in You, Lord (Psalm 40:2–3).

Add any of your own words . . .

CONFESS

There is no one like You, my God, who rides on the heavens to help me and on the clouds in Your majesty. You, Eternal God, are my refuge and underneath me are your everlasting arms. Drive out my enemy before me, Lord, saying "Destroy him!" (Deuteronomy 33:26, 27). Blessed am I! Who is like me, a person saved by the Lord? You are my shield and helper and glorious sword (Deuteronomy 33:29). Lord, may Your hand be ready to help me, for I am choosing Your precepts. I long for Your salvation, O Lord, and for Your law to be my delight. Let me live that I may praise You, and may Your laws sustain me. I have strayed like a lost sheep. Seek your servant, for I have not forgotten Your commands (Psalm 119:173–176).

Add any of your own words ...

CONSENT

God, You arm me with strength and make my way perfect. You can make my feet like the feet of a deer; You can enable me to stand on the heights. You train my hands for battle; my arms can bend a bow of bronze. You give me Your shield of victory; You stoop down to lift me up. You broaden the path beneath me, so that my ankles do not turn (2 Samuel 22:33–37). Nothing is too difficult for You, my God (Genesis 18:14). Into your hands I commit myself. Redeem me, O Lord, the God of truth (Psalms 31:5). Praise be to You, Lord, for showing Your wonderful love to me when I was besieged and felt cut off from Your sight. You heard my cry for mercy (Psalm 31:21–22).

Add any of your own words ...

TUESDAY

CRY OUT

To You, O Lord, I cry aloud and You will surely answer me from your holy hill (Psalm 3:4). Arise, O Lord! Deliver me, O my God! From You alone comes deliverance. May Your blessing be upon Your people (Psalm 3:4–5). May my cry come before You, O Lord; give me understanding according to Your Word. May my requests come before You; deliver me according to Your promise (Psalm 119:169–170). Lord, You are my light and my salvation—whom shall I fear? The Lord is the stronghold of my life—of whom shall I be afraid (Psalm 27:1). Make me confident of this: I will see the goodness of the Lord in the land of the living (Psalm 27:13). You have told me everything is possible for him who believes. Help me overcome my unbelief (Mark 9:23–24).

Add any of your own words . . .

CONFESS

Lord, help me discern my errors. Forgive my hidden faults. Keep your servant also from willful sins; may they not rule over me (Psalm 19:12–13a). Lord, You call me blessed because my transgressions are forgiven and my sins are covered. Blessed is the one whose sin the Lord does not count against him and in whose spirit is no deceit. Lord, when I kept silent and did not confess my sin to You, my bones wasted away through my groaning all day long. For day and night Your hand was heavy upon me; my strength was sapped as in the heat of summer. Help me to continue to acknowledge where I fall into sin and help me to count on Your unwavering forgiveness (Psalm 32:1–5).

Add any of your own words . . .

CONSENT

Lord, I know and I have heard that You are the everlasting God, the Creator of the ends of the earth. You will not grow tired or weary, and Your understanding no one can fathom. You give strength to the weary and increase the power of the weak. Even youths grow tired and weary, and young men stumble and fall; but those who hope in You will renew their strength. They will soar on wings like eagles; they will run and not grow weary, they will walk and not be faint (Isaiah 40:28–31). Lord, as You call upon my cooperation to be pulled out of this pit, help me to rest assured that I labor with all Your energy, which so powerfully works in me (Colossians 1:29). Your grace is sufficient for me, for Your power is made perfect in my weakness (2 Corinthians 12:9a).

Add any of your own words . . .

WEDNESDAY

CRY OUT

Out of the depths I cry to You, O Lord; O Lord, hear my voice. Let Your ears be attentive to my cry for mercy (Psalm 130:1–2). If I am in Christ and He is my Savior, I do not need to fear condemnation from You, Lord, because Your Word says that there is no condemnation for those of us who are in Christ Jesus (Romans 12:1). If You, O Lord, kept a record of sins, O Lord, who could stand? But with You there is forgiveness; therefore You are feared. I wait for You, my soul waits, and in Your Word I put my hope (Psalm 130:1–5). I want to clothe myself in humility before You and others, Lord, because You oppose the proud but give grace to the humble.

Add any of your own words . . .

CONFESS

Lord, enable me to put to death everything that belongs to my earthly nature: sexual immorality, impurity, lust, evil desires and greed, which is idolatry. I have walked in some of these ways, Lord, but with Your power, I can get rid of things like anger, rage, malice, slander, and filthy language from my lips. Help me not to lie, since I am taking off my old self with its practices and am putting on my new self, which is being renewed in knowledge in the image of its Creator (Colossians

3:5–10). I want to hold to Your teachings, Lord, and as I know the truth, the truth will set me free (John 8:31–32).

Add any of your own words . . .

CONSENT

Lord, please help me prepare my mind for action. Enable me to be self-controlled and set my hope fully on the grace to be given me when Jesus Christ is revealed (1 Peter 1:13–15). Lord, help me not to be downcast or disturbed from within. I can put my hope entirely in You, Lord, and I will keep praising You, my Savior and my God (Psalm 42:5). In all these things I am more than a conqueror through You, my God, who loves me. I am convinced that nothing can separate me from the love You have for me in Christ Jesus my Lord: neither death nor life, neither angels nor demons, neither the present nor future, nor any powers, neither height nor depth, nor anything else in all creation (Romans 8:37–39). You have never left me nor forsaken me (Hebrews 13:5). You are with me always (Matthew 28:20).

Add any of your own words . . .

THURSDAY

CRY OUT

Lord, Your Word says that if I call out for insight and cry aloud for understanding, and if I look for it as for silver and search for it as for hidden treasure, then I will understand the fear of the Lord and find the knowledge of God. For You give wisdom, and from Your mouth come knowledge and understanding (Proverbs 2:3–6). If I've reaped some consequences, Lord, help me not to despise Your discipline or resent Your rebuke. You discipline those You love, as a Father delights in His child (Proverbs 3:11–12). You are forgiving and good, O Lord, abounding in love to all who call to You. Hear my prayer, O Lord; listen to my cry for mercy (Psalm 86:5–6). You do not treat me as my sins would deserve (Psalm 103:10). As high as the heavens are above the earth, so great is Your love for those who fear You (Psalm 103:11).

Add any of your own words . . .

CONFESS

Jesus, You said that the person who hears Your words and puts them into practice is like a wise man who built his house on the rock. The rain came down, the streams rose, and the winds blew and beat against that house; yet it did not fall, because it had its foundation on the rock. But I have been like the person who heard Your words and did not put them into practice. At times I have been like a foolish man who built his house on sand. The rain has come down, the streams have risen, and the winds have blown and beat against my house. Parts of it have fallen with a great crash (Matthew 7:24–27). You can empower me to rebuild ancient ruins and raise up old foundations. I can become a repairer of broken walls (Isaiah 58:12). I will find joy in You, Lord, and ride on the heights once again and feast on my inheritance (Isaiah 58:14).

Add any of your own words . . .

CONSENT

Lord, with regard to my former way of life, You are helping me to put off my old self, which would only be corrupted by continued deceitful desires. Make me new in the attitude of my mind and help me to put on the new self, created to be like You in true righteousness and holiness (Ephesians 4:22–24). I want to offer my entire self to you as a living sacrifice, holy and pleasing to You, Lord. I will never find wholeness by conforming to this world. Help me to seek the transformation that comes by the renewing of my mind. Enable me to test and approve what Your will is for me, Lord. Your will for my life is good, pleasing, and perfect (Romans 12:1–2).

Add any of your own words . . .

FRIDAY

CRY OUT

Restore me, O God Almighty; make Your face shine upon me, that I may be delivered (Psalm 80:7). Answer me with awesome deeds of righteousness, O God my Savior (Psalm 65:5). My salvation and my honor depend on You, God; You are my mighty rock, my refuge (Psalm 62:7). Create in me a pure heart, O God, and renew a steadfast spirit within me. Thank you for the assurance I have in Christ that You will not ever cast me from Your presence or take Your Holy Spirit from me. Restore to me the joy of Your salvation and grant me a willing spirit, to sustain me (Psalm 51:10–12).

Add any of your own words . . .

CONFESS

I come to You, Jesus, weary and burdened. Please give me rest. I want to take Your yoke upon me and learn from You, for You are gentle and humble in heart. Let me find rest for my soul. For Your yoke is easy and Your burden is light (Matthew 11:28–30). Lord, You are faithful to all Your promises and loving toward all You have made. You uphold all those who fall and lift up all who are bowed down (Psalm 145:13b–14). Help me to trust in You at all times and pour out my heart to You for You are my refuge (Psalm 62:8). You, O God, are strong and You, O Lord, are loving (Psalm 62:11b).

Add any of your own words . . .

CONSENT

Father, when I was dead in my sins and in the uncircumcision of my sinful nature, You made me alive with Christ. You forgave me all my sins, having canceled the written code, with its regulations, that was against me and that stood opposed to me; You took it away, nailing it to the cross. And having disarmed the powers and authorities, You made a public spectacle of them, triumphing over them by the cross (Colossians 2:13–16). Therefore I am blessed with every spiritual blessing in Christ because You chose me in Him before the creation of the world to be holy and blameless in His sight. You predestined me to be adopted as Your child through Jesus Christ because it pleased You (Ephesians 1:3–5). Now, grant me the Spirit of wisdom and revelation that I may know You better (Ephesians 1:17). Help me to desire to do Your will, O my God. Put Your law within my heart (Psalm 40:8).

Add any of your own words . . .

SATURDAY

CRY OUT

Hear my cry, O God; listen to my prayer. From the ends of the earth I call to You, I call as my heart grows faint; lead me to the rock that is higher than I. For You have been my refuge, a strong tower against the foe. I long to dwell in Your tent forever and take refuge in the shelter of Your wings (Psalm 61:1–4). Show me Your glory, Lord (Exodus 33:18). Help me to keep my face continually unveiled before You and cause me to reflect that glory. Continue transforming me into Your likeness with ever-increasing glory, which comes from You, Lord (2 Corinthians 3:18).

Add any of your own words . . .

CONFESS:

Lord, help me to come near to You with my heart and not just my mouth. Help me honor You with more than my lips alone. Help me not hold my heart far from You. Open my eyes to any way that my worship of You has been made up only of rules taught by men (Isaiah 29:13). I want to worship You in Spirit and in truth, Lord (John 4:23). For where the Spirit of the Lord is, there is freedom (2 Corinthians 3:17). I have the treasure of Christ Himself in my jar of clay to show that this all-surpassing power is from God and not from me. I've been hard pressed on every side but I am not crushed. I am perplexed but not in despair; I may be persecuted but I am not abandoned. I've been struck down but I am not destroyed. Therefore I do not lose heart (2 Corinthians 4:7–9, 16a).

Add any of your own words . . .

CONSENT

My Father, how great is the love you have lavished on me, that I should be called a child of God. And that is what I am (1 John 3:1). Satisfy me in the morning with Your unfailing love, that I may sing for joy and be glad all my days (Psalm 90:14). Empower me to love You, Lord my God, with all my heart and with all my soul and with all my mind and with all my strength. Help me, God, to love others as I love myself (Mark 12:29–30). Empower me to forgive others as You forgive me (Matthew 6:12). Pour Your love into my heart (Romans 5:5) and help me to love my enemies (Luke 6:35). In suffering, help me commit myself to You, my faithful Creator, and continue to do good (1 Peter 4:19). Fill me with absolute confidence that You who began a good work in me will carry it on to completion until the day of Christ Jesus (Philippians 1:6).

Add any of your own words . . .

Get Out of That Pit
Discovery Guide

Each of these short studies is designed not only to enhance your learning and application of the ideas developed in *Get Out of That Pit*, but also to help you interact with the biblical passages that prompted those ideas, especially Psalm 40:1–3.

The first section of each study, "Reflection Questions," comes from one of the chapters in the book and will help you recall and review the main points of each chapter. Following each question is the page number from which you can find your answer.

The second section, "Personal Application," will help you personally apply the material by relating the lessons from each chapter to your own life.

Both sections of the Discovery Guide may be used by you individually or in a group discussion. If you are in a group, there will be time for you to share your "Personal Application" responses as you wish. You should not feel required to share unless you so desire.

You are encouraged to try to answer all the questions in the guide. The Holy Spirit uses your efforts as you seek to respond.

CHAPTER ONE
LIFE IN THE PIT

REFLECTION QUESTIONS

1. For some people, a pit can be so close they can't see it. Why is this true? (p. 8)

2. When Christ said, "Come, follow me," there was something else inherent in his invitation. What was it? (p. 7)

3. The amusing illustration of a person driving an RV into the living room of her new home makes an important point. What is it? (p. 10)

4. Often we don't recognize a pit when we're in one. What three signs characterize a pit? In other words, you know you're in a pit when... (pp. 14–19)

5. What is the difference between being in a pit with being in sin? (p. 20)

PERSONAL APPLICATION

1. From what you've learned in this chapter, would you say you're now—or have been—in a pit? Describe how that feels—or felt at the time.

2. Have you ever been—or are you now—a "mobile pit dweller"? If so, what was/is the nature of your mobile pit, and where did/do you take it?

3. "The close confinement of a pit exhausts us with the endless echo of self-absorption." Do you resonate with this statement? If so, why?

4. "Some of us recognize our pits, not by the degree of our badness, but by the degree of our boredom." Reflect on the "degree of boredom" in your own life and whether or not it's an indication that you may be in a pit.

5. What hope do the words of Psalm 40 offer you personally in terms of the pit you may be in?

CHAPTER TWO
YOU GET THROWN IN

REFLECTION QUESTIONS

1. We can be thrown into "pits of innocence." Give some examples of ways innocent people are thrown into pits. (pp. 25–28)

2. A pit we are thrown into can be the most complicated to deal with, emotionally and spiritually. Why? (p. 29)

3. Sometimes we start out in a pit of innocence, but later find ourselves in a pit of sin. What is the potential sin of a person who has been thrown into a pit? (p. 32)

4. Forgiveness is not about feeling or passivity. What is it about? (p. 33)

5. Holding God ultimately responsible in the *healthy way* His Word suggests will be our ticket out of a pit. What is this healthy way? Read Genesis 50:20 to discover how Joseph found a healthy way to hold God responsible. (p. 42)

PERSONAL APPLICATION

1. If someone has thrown you into a pit of innocence, where are you now, in terms of getting out and finding that "firm place to stand" the psalmist talked about? Stuck in the mud and mire? Working your way out? Standing on a rock? Explain your answer.

2. Have you ever felt "comfortable" living in a pit? If so, why was this true for you at the time?

3. Has the "willingness" and "power" of forgiveness ever been something you have experienced? If so, describe the circumstances and the outcome.

4. "We can be in a pit innocently even if we haven't always been innocent." What does this statement mean to you, in terms of our feelings of guilt?

5. "Your wealth of experience makes you rich. Spend it on people." How might God use your own suffering to help or heal others?

CHAPTER THREE
YOU CAN SLIP IN

REFLECTION QUESTIONS

1. What are several ways a person might slip into a pit? (pp. 55–57)

2. What is Satan's three-step progressive plan to get us to slip into a pit? (p. 60)

3. Scripture has a name for a small distraction that becomes a big distraction. What is it? (p. 61)

4. What is the Christian's built-in "alarm system" against slipping into sin? How does that alarm system work in a person's life? (p. 65)

5. Read 1 John 4:4. What does this verse say about the possibility of Satan's trapping you into staying in a pit? (p. 65)

PERSONAL APPLICATION

1. Read Psalm 38: 4–6, 9, 12, and 14–17. Think of a time when you slid into a pit, and underline the words in those verses that describe how you felt (or feel now) about the situation in which you found (or find) yourself.

2. If you were in Christ at the time of Satan's first distraction, when did the Holy Spirit first sound an alarm? How did you respond?

3. What are some tricks Satan uses to distract you into sliding into sin?

4. Are you now in the "distraction" phase of a potential pit? If so, what is the Holy Spirit saying to you? What do you need to do *now*?

5. Are you now in the "addiction" phase of a pit? Read 1 John 4:4 again and reflect on what it means in your situation. What do you need to do to claim that promise?

CHAPTER FOUR
YOU CAN JUMP IN

REFLECTION QUESTIONS

1. The third way we can get into a pit is by jumping in. How does this method differ from the other two, especially in terms of the motive and mindset of the person who jumps? (p. 71)

2. Why is "jumping in" the most dangerous and supremely consequential method of getting into a pit? (p. 76)

3. What is a "deformed desire"? (p. 80)

4. How does the Holy Spirit warn us against "forbidden relationships"? (p. 85)

5. What one word does God use as His quickest way to shove us away from a pit? (p. 85)

PERSONAL APPLICATION

1. "We are so perfectly fitted for passion that we will find it one way or another. If we don't find it in Christ, we'll find it in things like lust, anger, rage, and greed." How have you seen this truth displayed in your own life or those you know?

2. Each of us will ultimately do what we want to do. Christ asks, "What do you want, Child?" How will you answer that question?

3. The psalmist said, "I delight to do Your will, O my God: Your law is within my heart" (Psalm 40:8 NASB). On a continuum between "not at all" to "yes, I'm there," how true is this for you today?

4. A Barbie doll with one foot gnawed off provided a poignant image for Beth's spiritual condition. What image would you use to describe *your* spiritual status as you think about your own propensity toward pit jumping?

5. Why is God wise to never let you forget the excruciating pain of where you've been?

CHAPTER FIVE
YOU CAN GET OUT

REFLECTION QUESTIONS

1. We can get out of our pit, but not alone or with human help. What will it take? (p. 91)

2. If a man—or a woman—assumes the sole role of our deliverer, what will he or she inadvertently do? (p. 93)

3. People can "help us," "lift us," and on occasion "pull us" out of a pit, but what can't they do? (p. 92)

4. Why do some people abandon their hurting friends? (p. 99)

5. If we can't pull someone out of a pit, what are five things we can do to "affect profound change in someone's life"? (pp. 105–106)

PERSONAL APPLICATION

1. By now, you've probably identified one or more pits you have been in. How have you been trying to "deal" with them up until now?

2. What practical steps can you take to address the limitations of your friends, family members, professional counselor, minister, and support group?

3. Are you angry with someone in your life whom you have felt or feel has let you down? What role can forgiveness play in helping you to heal the hurt feelings?

4. What does Philippians 1:6 and 2 Corinthians 1:10 tell us about God's faithfulness? Which words in these verses mean the most to you personally, and why?

5. Is there someone in your life you've been attempting to rescue? If so, how do you think you should relate to his or her problem from now on?

CHAPTER SIX
YOU CAN OPT FOR GOD

REFLECTION QUESTIONS

1. You can opt for God. What provisions do the Father, the Son, and the Holy Spirit provide that qualify them to pull someone out of a pit? (pp. 113–114)

2. What are the three steps the Bible proposes for getting out of the pit? Say them out loud. If you're in a group, say them LOUD. (p. 119)

3. Describe the kind of crying out a pit dweller has to do. Why does God usually wait for us to cry out before rescuing us? (pp. 120–122)

4. After we cry out, confess. What does our confession include? (p. 126)

5. After we confess, consent. What does consent mean in this case? To what must we consent? (p. 131)

PERSONAL APPLICATION

1. In order to get out of your pit, "God wants everything you've got. Uncontested priority. Every egg in one basket. All your weight on one limb." What would have to happen in your life for you to take this challenge seriously?

2. If you are ready to begin your ascent from the pit, what words would you use to cry out to God?

3. What do you need to confess to God? What attitude, motive, and action can you think of that contributed to your being in a pit?

4. What will it mean for you to "actively consent" to getting out of your pit?

5. Turn now to the "Scripture Prayers" section in the back of this book. Plan to spend one week reading aloud the "cry out, confess, and consent" prayers for each day. Continue to use these prayers as long as you are waiting for God to lift you out of your pit.

CHAPTER SEVEN
WAITING ON GOD
FOR DELIVERANCE

REFLECTION QUESTIONS

1. God is driven by relationship. In terms of getting out of a pit, what is His part, and what is our part? (p. 147)

2. Most of the time we have to wait patiently for deliverance from our pits, but during the wait what are some things for which we never have to wait? (p. 149)

3. What are some signs that our deliverance process is well under way? (p. 149)

4. Read Psalm 40:1–2. What is the true meaning of the Hebrew term (*qwh*) that we translate as "wait"? Describe a person who is waiting for the Lord as the Hebrew psalmist meant it. (p. 150)

5. Read Psalm 130:1–6. What does this Psalm add that shows the posture or attitude of someone waiting for God? (p. 152)

PERSONAL APPLICATION

1. God can deliver a person instantaneously, but this is a rare occurrence. Has this ever happened to you or to someone you know? What was your response? Were you awed by God's power? Skeptical? Reassured?

2. As you have waited for God to deliver you, what has been your frame of mind? Compare yours with the psalmists' in Psalm 40:1-2 and 130:5-6.

3. "But smooth living invariably, eventually, makes for sloppy spirituality." Can you think of a time in your life when this was especially true?

4. Psalm 130:5 says, "in his word I put my hope." In the past, where have you placed your hope? What is one thing you can do while you wait and hope for deliverance?

5. Another definition of *qwh* (wait) is "to bind together." As you picture Beth's two children clinging to her legs, describe yourself as you have begun to hold on to God.

CHAPTER EIGHT
MAKE UP YOUR MIND

REFLECTION QUESTIONS

1. If we want to get out of a pit for good, what is the one absolutely crucial thing we must do? (p. 161)

2. In order to stay out of a pit, why is it important to have certain questions answered before life asks them; some things settled in advance of the inevitable temptation to revert or destructively scratch a temporary itch. (p. 163)

3. Why is staying out of a pit, while others close to us are still in one, the biggest challenge of all? (p. 168)

4. When God performs a dramatic deliverance in our lives, what are some of the changes we can expect in our relationships? (p. 176)

5. Why do some relationships need to end, not just change? (p. 177)

PERSONAL APPLICATION

1. What are some of the inevitable temptations you can expect to face in the next few days, weeks, or months as you attempt to stand firmly on your rock?

2. "We must settle some things in advance." When the next temptations arise, what might you say or do differently that indicate you have "made up your mind"?

3. Which relationship(s) in your life will have to change as a result of your resolve to stay out of the pit? How will your family change? How will your relationships with friends change?

4. Is there a relationship in your life that is fueled by addiction or is in danger of becoming so? Is this a relationship that you must end? Why or why not?

5. When you say goodbye to your pit once and for all, you'll "live in the fresh air and sunshine." Describe what that will look like and feel like in your life.

CHAPTER NINE
SINGING A NEW SONG

REFLECTION QUESTIONS

1. Right after God sets us on the rock and gives us a firm place to stand, what, according to Psalm 40:3, is the very next thing he does? (p. 183)

2. "Your heart beats to the rhythm of a God-song, and your vocal chords were fashioned to give it volume." What is a God-song? (p. 183)

3. If having a new song in our mouths does not mean we are completely free from pain, what does it mean? (p. 190)

4. How can we know the songs of heaven are unceasingly sung as accompaniment on our journey out of the pit? (p. 194)

5. Until we get to heaven where we'll hear God's actual songs that will accompany our deliverance, what should we do? How do we sing? (p. 196)

PERSONAL APPLICATION

1. Have you begun to hear a God-song in your heart? Can you put words to your song? If it is an actual song that you can sing, sing it!

2. Describe a time when you spontaneously began singing a song of praise—maybe in your car, at home, in an elevator, etc. Also describe a time when you sang, not because you felt like it, but as an act of faith. What was the result of your singing?

3. When you're in a pit, you may be singing a song, but it's usually not a God-song. What are some of the enemy's songs that you've been singing? If you can't think of an actual song, make up a song title that fits your situation. (Think country, and have fun with this!)

4. Now, pick one or two songs and/or soundtracks that you think God might use to accompany your victorious deliverance from a pit. If you don't have these CDs at home, buy or borrow them this week and play them every day.

5. This week, find a time and place where there will be no other distractions. Then play the music you've chosen while picturing in your mind the dramatic moment of your victory over the deadly pit from which you're now emerging (or soon will be).

CHAPTER TEN
OUR PIT-LESS FUTURE

REFLECTION QUESTIONS

1. According to Revelation 21:1–6, what will eventually happen to the world (the first earth) as we know it? What will replace it? (p. 204)

2. Comparing Psalm 23:1–3 with Revelation 7:17, how will life in Heaven be different from life on earth? (pp. 204–205)

3. At the end of time, what happens to Satan, according to Revelation 20:1–3? (p. 206)

4. In God's economy, what happens to those who dig a pit for others? (p. 206)

5. What does Romans 8:18 promise us, in terms of our present suffering? (p. 207)

PERSONAL APPLICATION

1. What comes to mind when you try to answer the question, "What's this world coming to?"

2. When you read Revelation 21:1–4, what are your feelings? Describe how your life might one day be—without pain or tears.

3. Have you decided to take the hand of Christ and be released from your pit? If not, do it now by praying a prayer, giving your life to Him and asking Him to be your Savior *and* Lord.

4. Make a list of the most important things you've learned while reading this book.

5. What specific decisions have you made that will help you get out of your pit? Write them down and put your list in a prominent place as inspiration for your victorious life—out of the pit!

Beth Moore founded
Living Proof Ministries
upon Hebrews 4:12.

For the Word of God is living and active.
Sharper than any two edged sword.

All who serve within the doors of LPM
share her passion to see every individual
come to love and live on God's Word.

Each tape, book and product offered
through this ministry is developed to
encourage people to know Jesus Christ
and to respond to His love
with holy passion.

Thank you for giving us the privilege
to serve Christ through serving you.

BETH MOORE PRESENTS:
SONGS OF
DELIVERANCE

Music inspired by the book *Get Out of That Pit*

BETH MOORE PRESENTS: SONGS OF DELIVERANCE is the companion CD to Beth's inspiring new book *Get Out of That Pit – Straight Talk about God's Deliverance*. An all-star cast of Christian recording artists sing their own stories of deliverance that echo the themes of the book:

AMY GRANT

STEVEN CURTIS CHAPMAN

CECE WINANS

WYNONNA

SARA GROVES

JOY WILLIAMS

MANDISA

TRAVIS COTTRELL

RONNIE FREEMAN

PAUL BALOCHE

indelible
creative group

www.indelibleonline.com

ALSO from BETH MOORE

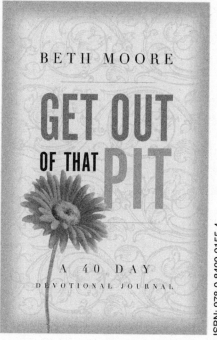

In this companion devotional journal, Beth Moore continues to point people to the deliverance that awaits from the One who can rescue them completely. The scriptures, thought-provoking questions, prayers, and room for reflection will assure fellow travelers that no matter how they got stuck, no matter how long they've been down, whether they think they deserve it or not, their Redeemer is waiting.

AVAILABLE WHEREVER BOOKS ARE SOLD

THOMAS NELSON
Since 1798

For other products and live events,
visit us at: thomasnelson.com